PETER HARRISON

First American Architect

FIGURE 1. The tower at the west end of King's Chapel, Boston, showing Peter Harrison's use of a façade architecture. The colonnade was added by Thomas Clement, 1785-1787, who is said to have followed the original plans faithfully except in the substitution of wood for stone.

Peter Harrison

FIRST AMERICAN ARCHITECT

BY

CARL BRIDENBAUGH

PUBLISHED FOR
THE INSTITUTE OF
EARLY AMERICAN HISTORY
AND CULTURE
AT WILLIAMSBURG, VIRGINIA

Chapel Hill, 1949

THE UNIVERSITY OF NORTH CAROLINA PRESS

For

A. LAWRENCE KOCHER

Preface

AS THE eighteenth century came to an end, thoughtful Americans like Thomas Jefferson and the Reverend Samuel Miller gravely pondered the role that their countrymen had played in the brilliant achievements of the Enlightenment. Almost pathetically they ransacked the states to uncover among the people of the new nation exemplars of the arts and sciences whose accomplishments were sufficiently notable to warrant inclusion in the company of the century's great men. In statesmanship Americans stood in the front rank; in science their record was creditable; but in the fine arts they could boast few names worthy of the notice of posterity.

Prior to the War for Independence two colonials had earned a place with the "luminaries of the eighteenth century"—John Singleton Copley in painting and Peter Harrison of Newport in architecture. Yet neither in the *Notes on Virginia* (1782) nor in *A Brief Retrospect of the Eighteenth Century* (1803) can one find any mention of Peter Harrison, and one is led to ask why he has been so long forgotten.

There was dire need for artists in the Young Republic. A new and radical experiment in government was under way, and the eyes of the Western World were focused upon America. Could the arts flourish and attain perfection without aristocratic patronage, demanded the skeptics of monarchial Europe. The only answer was the development of a new art, and, especially, a new architecture expressive of republican virtue.

Despite the fact that every one of Peter Harrison's buildings survived the Revolution—and in fact is still standing—patriots dared not adduce as proof of their artistic maturity the work of a Tory tarred with the additional odium of service in the King's Customs. Thomas Jefferson, moreover, never traveled to Rhode Island or Massachusetts, and went to his grave ignorant of the fact that Peter Harrison had anticipated him in the revival of classical models. He never knew that the loyalist was his precursor in the evolution of a new, pure form of architecture that would reflect the republicanism of the New World.

When the passions born of conflict subsided and historians turned to the study of the Tories, Peter Harrison remained in oblivion because a New Haven mob had totally destroyed his papers and drawings. Consequently, any study of the man and his work has to be made from stray materials found in the correspondence of other persons of his time. This biographical essay—for it cannot be termed a full-dress biography—is thus the fruit of accidental research undertaken over a long period of years. There are many gaps in this story of Peter Harrison and his buildings, but I believe that I have presented the broad outlines and most significant aspects of his career. Because so little is known about any of the colonial architects, it seems fitting to publish this account of the first great American designer on the two hundredth anniversary of the completion of his plan for King's Chapel at Boston.

The illustrations are an integral and indispensable part of this book, and have been arranged to facilitate their use in connection with the text. Figures that are mentioned in the discussion of particular buildings and Peter Harrison's bookish sources are grouped together near the end of the volume, while those that bear more directly upon his life are inserted at appropriate places in the text. The captions are intended to amplify the text and assist the reader in relating the illustrations to the discussion of the buildings.

No author could have succeeded in his quest for materials about Peter Harrison without the generous and interested assistance of many friends and, perhaps even more, of persons to whom he was a complete stranger. I am privileged to be able to record my gratitude to all of them.

When I first seriously began to investigate the career of Peter Harrison, Miss Mary T. Quinn, efficient custodian of the Rhode Island State Archives at Providence, discovered documents that made further progress possible. Mrs. Peter Bolhouse, Leonard Panaggio, and Herbert Brigham of the Newport Historical Society industriously searched for items I could not find during my several visits to Newport. Mr. Maurice P. Van Buren of New York City placed his collection of Harrison materials at my disposal without restriction, thoughtfully presented the Institute with photostatic copies of the only remaining letters of his ancestor, and enabled me to have photographs of the portraits of the Harrisons.

Miss Mary S. Batchelder of Cambridge, with rare graciousness, gathered notes and other papers of her brother, the late Samuel Francis Batchelder, and gave me unrestricted access to them. Mr. Batchelder's papers, the fruit of twenty-five years of research on Peter Harrison, proved invaluable to me.

The Reverend Henry Wilder Foote of Cambridge, who has identified Nathaniel Smibert as the painter of the Harrison portraits, kindly communicated this information to me when this book was in galley proof.

The following individuals and institutions assisted me in uncovering materials: Frank Malloy Anderson of Hanover; Miss Helen Boatfield and Mrs. Robert C. Bruch of New Haven; Mrs. Eleanor J. Brackett and Miss Frances Hubbert of the Redwood Library, Newport; Professor Dora Mae Clark of Wilson College; Antoinette Downing of Providence; Hunter Dupree of Cambridge; the late Allyn Bailey Forbes and Stephen T. Riley of the Massachusetts Historical Society; John H. Greene, Jr., of the Newport County Court; Brooke Hindle of Williamsburg; the Reverend Palfrey Perkins of King's Chapel, Boston; Granville Prior of the Citadel, Charleston; Clifford K. Shipton of Shirley; St. George L. Sioussat of Chevy Chase; and Walter Muir Whitehill of the Boston Athenaeum.

Also, the officials of the Avery Library at Columbia University; the Library of the College of William and Mary; the Connecticut State Library at Hartford; the Harvard University Library; the Historical Society of Pennsylvania; the Henry E. Huntington Library and Art Gallery at San Marino; the Library of Congress; the Mariner's Museum at Newport News; the New Hampshire Historical Society at Concord; the New York Public Library; the Rhode Island Historical Society at Providence; and the Yale University Library, placed every facility at my disposal.

Roberta H. Bridenbaugh, Douglass Adair, and Lester J. Cappon have read the manuscript in its several drafts and have suggested many improvements, both in organization and style. A. Edwin Kendrew, William S. Perry, and Fiske Kimball have generously aided me in architectural matters, while Mrs. William Phelan and Miss Margaret Kinard rendered great assistance with the manuscript.

My greatest debt is to A. Lawrence Kocher, who not only allowed me to use his unrivalled library of eighteenth-century architectural books, but patiently guided an importunate novice through the maze of architectural history and saved him from making many blunders. To him I have ventured to dedicate this book.

CARL BRIDENBAUGH

Williamsburg, Virginia
1 October, 1948

Contents

Illustrations

Note: Most of the photographs of buildings shown in the illustrations were taken by the Historic American Buildings Survey and are reproduced through the courtesy of the Library of Congress. The photographs of King's Chapel were made by Arthur C. Haskell of Marblehead, Massachusetts.

PETER HARRISON

First American Architect

From Quarter Deck to Counting House

NEWPORT, "the Metropolitan of Southern New England," buzzed with excitement on the brisk morning of December 2, 1763. Despite the little city's not altogether complimentary reputation as "the receptacle of all religious opinions," its atmosphere vibrated with eager expectancy as the time drew near for the dedication of what the local bard called "a Synagogue of Satan"—the second Hebrew Temple to be erected in America. And why not? The edifice had been a-building ever since August, 1759, when Mr. Aaron Lopez had laid the first cornerstone.

To the Reverend Ezra Stiles, minister of the Second Congregational Church and librarian of the Redwood Library, this was a great occasion indeed. Tolerant in his religious views, this universal scholar attended the afternoon ceremonies in a frame of mind far transcending that of his notoriously curious Yankee fellow-townsmen. He was wonderfully impressed. So, also, was the printer of the *Newport Mercury*, who covered the assignment. "The Order and Decorum," he reported, "the Harmony and Solemnity of the Musick, together with a Handsome Assembly of People, in an Edifice the most perfect of the Temple Kind perhaps in America, and splendidly illuminated, could not but raise in the Mind a faint Idea of the Majesty and Grandeur of the Ancient Jewish Worship mentioned in Scripture. Dr. Isaac de Abraham Touro performed the Service." After carefully copying this notice in his diary, Mr. Stiles appended a meticulous description of the salient architectural features of the little building. Significantly, he failed to record the name of the architect of the Synagogue—the man who had also planned Stiles's beloved Redwood Library.[1] Nor was the designer accorded any recognition by the press. We do not even know whether he was present at the ceremonies.

The Synagogue had been designed by Peter Harrison, a prominent and public-spirited resident of Newport. From that day until this his has been a shadowy figure. Probably Ezra Stiles and the printer deemed mention of his name or presence unnecessary. Moreover, in the eighteenth century architects did not occupy the position now enjoyed by successful members of their profession. Peter Harrison had only recently arrived at a gentleman's estate; with him a knowledge of architecture and design was a gentle accomplishment, not the basis of a profession. Perhaps he shrank somewhat self-consciously from publicity as unworthy of one of his dignity and station, but, at any rate, until recently all accounts of Peter Harrison have been compounded of local tradition, erroneous conjectures, and some genuinely remarkable suppositions.[2] In consequence, historians have so generally ignored his existence that no mention of his work is made in the leading histories of the colonies. Who was Peter Harrison?

1. *Newport Mercury*, Dec. 5, 1763; Franklin B. Dexter, ed., *The Literary Diary of Ezra Stiles* (New York, 1901), I, 6, *6n.*

2. In 1916 the first accurate accounts of Harrison appeared in two articles: Samuel F. Batchelder, "Peter Harrison," Society for the Preservation of New England Antiquities, *Bulletin*, 6, no. 2, pp. 12-29; and Charles H. Hart, "Peter Harrison, Architect," Massachusetts Historical Society, *Proceedings*, 49, pp. 261-68. These writers effectively disposed of the myth that Harrison worked with Sir John Vanbrugh at Blenheim, although a Newport writer repeated it as recently as 1936. The most satisfactory sketch is by Fiske Kimball in the *Dictionary of American Biography*, VIII, 347.

Peter Harrison's career is a colonial version of the American success story. It is the tale of a rather diffident lad destined to be a nobody in the England of his day, who, through the enterprise and social maneuvering of his ambitious older brother, was enabled to mature his talents across the Atlantic, to marry into one of the leading families of New England, and to become America's first important architect.

Because architecture was practiced almost exclusively by middle-class craftsmen and had not as yet developed into a recognized profession, very little is known about the early careers of English architects who lived in the seventeenth and eighteenth centuries. Just as this was true of Sir Christopher Wren and his contemporaries, so also was it the case with colonial designers, including Peter Harrison. He was born on June 14, 1716, the youngest of the four children of Elizabeth Dennyson and Thomas Harrison, Jr., Quaker folk of York in Old England.[3] For nearly six decades Peter and his brother Joseph, seven years his senior, were intimately associated; between them arose a notable affection, a mutual respect, and a capacity for working together not always present in fraternal undertakings. Age and temperament fitted the elder

3. The family tree in Appendix A has been prepared from the Harrison Papers now owned by Mr. Maurice P. Van Buren of New York City, a descendant, who generously placed them at my disposal. See also, Collections of the Genealogical Society of Pennsylvania: Quarterly Meeting of Yorkshire, Births, A-L, in Historical Society of Pennsylvania. According to his brother-in-law John Banister, when Peter Harrison arrived at Newport in 1739 he "wa'nt above 18 or 19." (Banister to Thomas Lee, Jan. 13, 1748/9, Banister Letter Book, 1748, Newport Historical Society.) If Banister was correct, Harrison must have been born in 1720 or 1721. Although the Family Tree gives no source for the date June 14, 1716, it was accepted by an English Court at the York Assizes, July 30, 1822, in the case of Doe v. Acklam (4 *Dowling and Rylands*, 394), *English Reports: King's Bench Division*, 107 (London, 1910), 572-79. This date more nearly accords with the dates of birth of the other members of the family. Peter would thus have been twenty-three on his arrival at Rhode Island, an age that makes his several accomplishments more credible than in a lad of nineteen.

brother to head the partnership and also the family when the father died in 1736.[4]

Like most Quakers, the Harrisons provided their sons with a sound elementary education which was reflected in later years in fine handwriting, in the clarity and correctness of their letters, and in the development of a bookishness not usually noted among men of their station. As regular attendants at the York meeting the parents also accepted the religious ethic of George Fox, who exhorted all Friends to "train up your children in the fear of God, ... and as they are capable, they may be instructed and kept employed in some lawful calling, that they may be diligent, serving the Lord in the things that are good." [5] Accordingly both Joseph and Peter were brought up to a trade.

Although far from affluent the Harrisons were a family of considerable respectability whose ancestral heath was the seigniory of Holderness in the East Riding of Yorkshire. There they enjoyed the generous and friendly patronage of the Acklams, Lords of the Manor of Hornsea, a tiny market village situated between Hornsea Mere and the North Sea sixteen miles northeast of Hull. When, as young boys, Peter and Joseph visited at Hornsea, the manor house was presided over by Peter and Isabelle Acklam, for whom they came to have a lasting fondness.[6] Often present was Jonathan

4. Francis Drake, *Eboracum, or the History and Antiquities of the City of York* (London, 1736), 355, 364-65; Appendix liv-lvi. According to the Family Tree Thomas Harrison died in 1737, a discrepancy doubtless due to the fact that the death occurred on Feb. 1, 1736/7.

5. Quoted by Frederick B. Tolles, in "Benjamin Franklin's Business Mentors: The Philadelphia Quaker Merchants," *William and Mary Quarterly*, 3d ser., 4 (1947), 65.

6. Peter was probably named for Peter Acklam, and one of his daughters, Isabelle, after Mrs. Acklam. Members of the Harrison family, denied burial in the church yard because they were Quakers, were interred in the Acklam family plot at the "Low Hall." By Peter's time, however, the Acklams appear to have returned to the Anglican fold. George Poulson, *The History and Antiquities of the Seigniory of Holderness* (Hull, 1840-41), I, ix, 315-16, 316n., 329, 333-34; Thomas Allen, *History of the County of York* (London, 1831), IV, 218-19.

Acklam, High Sheriff of Nottinghamshire and client of the Duke of Newcastle, who took a liking to the brothers and frequently invited them down to his fine estate at Wyeston, near Bawtry.[7]

At Wyeston and Hornsea Peter and Joseph were introduced to a mode of life that contrasted oddly with the routine of plainness and practical training for worldly success inculcated by the Quaker environment at York. They readily absorbed the social ideals of the landed gentry and began to long for the status which lack of wealth and gentle birth denied them. The ease with which these qualities rose to the surface when the Harrisons came over to the New World, facilitating a quick and effortless, though definitely sincere, transition from Quaker simplicity to the social distinction and elaborate ritualism of the Church of England, is evidence of an attitude of life well ingrained from childhood. As an adult Peter Harrison exhibited a quiet dignity, a proud sense of position, a dilettantism, a cultivated taste, a love of pomp, and a devotion to the land that stemmed not from membership in the Society of Friends nor residence in the urban centers of Yorkshire.

Whatever his dreams, whatever his aspirations, England held little promise for a young man of his status in society. To cross the line into the gentry was next to impossible. Besides there was a living to be made, and like many another lad from Holderness Peter sought to make his fortune at sea.

"There is more Business done in Hull," Daniel Defoe observed in 1726, "than in any town of its bigness in Europe." It was the collecting and distributing center for the North of England, and ships from the Humber engaged in the Baltic, Norwegian, Dutch, French, and Spanish trades. Hull-built ships trafficked extensively

---

7. Bawtry was situated on the Idle River, which flows into the Trent, which in turn joins the Humber above Hull. On Wyeston and Bawtry, located in northern Nottinghamshire, close to the Yorkshire border, see H. Gill and E. L. Guilford, eds., *The Rector's Book of Clayworth, Notts* (Nottingham, 1910), 138-39, 144; for Jonathan Acklam, Poulson, *Holderness*, I, 454.

along the coast and also ventured into the whale fishery at Green-land.[8] At Hull Peter Harrison, like Joseph before him, learned the mystery of shipbuilding and the ways of the sea under the guidance of merchants connected with the Acklams. Chief among these was Christopher Scott, who, in partnership with John Thomlinson, a Yorkshire merchant at London, was reaching out for a trade with the colonies. There is some evidence to indicate that before 1738 Joseph Harrison had made at least one voyage in the mast trade to the Piscataqua for Thomlinson and Scott, and that through the good offices of the Acklams he had secured an introduction to the Wentworths and others of the merchant oligarchy at Portsmouth.[9] The elder Harrison, it seems, never lacked connections, nor was he wanting in the address and skill to exploit them.

By the time the Brothers Harrison reached manhood they had succeeded in demonstrating to their friends and sponsors that they were industrious young men of promise worth backing. In 1738 Joseph had risen to command of a ship fitted out by London merchants, and Peter had made at least one voyage with him. Lacking gentle birth, inherited lands, or wealth, they sought to make

8. "In a word, all the Trade at Leeds, Wakefield, and Hallifax, . . . is transacted here, and the Goods are ship'd here by Merchants of Hull; all the Lead Trade of Derbyshire and Nottinghamshire, from Bawtry Wharf, the Butter of the East and North Riding, brought down the Ouse to York; the Cheese brought down the Trent from Stafford, Warwick and Cheshire, and the Corn from all the Counties adjacent, are brought and ship'd off here." G. D. H. Cole, ed., Daniel Defoe, *A Tour through the Whole Island of Britain* (London, 1927), II, 654-55.

9. John Thomlinson was active in the mast trade from New Hampshire. He "understood the ways of access to the great," and at this very moment was intriguing at London to procure the appointment of Benning Wentworth (of Yorkshire connections) as the first separate governor of that province. Some Acklams had been in Portsmouth as early as 1715, and, in 1737, a "J. Harrison" had been among the "Strangers" who protested to the Selectmen against being taxed in each of the two parishes of the town. J. W. Hammond, ed., *Documents Relating to Towns in New Hampshire*, in *New Hampshire Provincial Papers* (Concord, 1882), XIII, 251; *Acts of the Privy Council, Colonial Series* (London, 1908), III, 592-93, 598-99, 630, 637; Jeremy Belknap, *History of New Hampshire* (Boston, 1813), II, 143.

their way in commerce in the good old eighteenth-century fashion, always trusting that by a turn of fortune they might better themselves and rise in the social scale. That they were on the make, social climbers and fortune hunters if you will, is the key to their careers.

John Banister, a "very eminent merchant" of Newport, on Rhode Island, crossed to London in 1738 to appear before the Privy Council in a case involving some Massachusetts lands belonging to rich old Edward Pelham, whose daughter, Hermione, Banister had married the year before. He also improved this opportunity by investigating possibilities for a direct trade between Newport and the mother country as well as traffic to the ports of the Baltic. To John Thomlinson he communicated his "Resonable Scheeme of settling a Ship in the Trade" between Newport and London, which, he declared, all Rhode Islanders "seeme fully Convinc'd is the only method to make them selves Independant of the [Massachusetts] Bay government, to whom they have a mortal aversion." [10]

Several London merchants trading to New England eagerly entered into this "Scheeme," particularly since colonial payments were to be made largely in Narragansett-built ships which were widely recognized as superior in quality to the "New England built" vessels sold at Boston. Through John Thomlinson's introduction John Banister came to visit Peter Acklam at Hornsea and to meet Jonathan Acklam of Wyeston, with whom he later stayed.

10. Thomas Banister, father of John, had been a prominent merchant of Boston, and had married in England, about 1704, a sister of "my Lady Say and Sele." This alliance, the fame of his father's *Essay on Trade* (London, 1715), and the Pelham connection naturally procured Banister the proper entrées at London. *Acts of the Privy Council*, III, 459, 498, 573-74; *Rhode Island Historical Magazine*, 6 (1885), 19; Banister to Capt. John Thomlinson, June 1, 1739; to Thomas Hall, June 20, 1739, Banister Letter Book, 1739; Gertrude S. Kimball, ed., *Correspondence of the Colonial Governors of Rhode Island* (Providence, 1902), I, 97-98.

It was either at Hornsea or in the counting house of Christopher Scott at Hull that the merchant first encountered the young master whose fortunes were to be linked with his. A decade later at Newport, Banister recalled that "in the year 1738 Joseph Harrison solicited me to freight his vessell for this Port, which I finally Concented too." [11] With the groundwork for a lucrative traffic thus laid John Banister sailed homeward.

Meanwhile, at London, Captain Joseph Harrison made ready the *Sheffield*, a ship of "140 tons or there abouts," for her first voyage to Newport. Sailing was delayed from February 10 to March 5, 1738/9, and then the vessel rode at the Downs awaiting favorable winds until March 10. At sea some days later the *Sheffield* met with a hard gale whose force required all of the efforts and skill of the master and his crew of ten—among whom was Peter Harrison—to keep her afloat and save her cargo from serious damage. After almost eight weeks on the tempestuous North Atlantic, Brenton's Reef was sighted to starboard on April 29, and almost before those on board were aware of it the storm-tossed vessel stood past Beavertail and Goat Island into Newport Harbor. Captain Harrison tied up at Pelham's Wharf and prepared to land his cargo of "European Goods fit for the Season," which, however, was partially "spoilt by Wind and Wave." The truth of this the master "affirmed" the next day when he made out the customary ship's protest, "he being one of the people called Quakers." [12]

After filing the protest Joseph and Peter Harrison repaired to Banister's counting house on Pelham's Wharf. "This Peter was Cabin boye or Reather a Steward," the merchant averred ten years later after he and Peter had fallen out. "He was a lad that

11. Banister to Thomas Lee, Jan. 13, 1748/9, Banister Letter Book, 1748.
12. Letters to the Governor of Rhode Island, 1731-41, pp. 44, 49, Rhode Island Archives, Providence; Kimball, *Correspondence*, I, 103-4; for the protest, Rhode Island Land Records, IV, 399-400, R. I. Archives; Banister Letter Book, 1739, p. 1.

engaged my fancy and I took Notice of him. Several things In-
ducing, principally I thot Jo. Treated him Sevearly. On arrival
at Newport I Introduced both brothers to my Father's house,
with whom I then lived." [13]

Thus on their first appearance at Rhode Island the two Quakers
gained an immediate access to the home of Edward Pelham, Banister's Anglican father-in-law. In point of family the Pelhams
were second to few in the American colonies. Mr. Pelham, grand-
son of the first treasurer of Harvard College, a gentleman of
taste and ample fortune, came of the same line as the Duke of
Newcastle. He was one of the few colonials who had never
worked for a living. His wife, Arabella Williams Pelham, grand-
daughter of Governor Benedict Arnold of Rhode Island, and her
two unmarried daughters, Elizabeth and Penelope, joined with
the Banisters and Mr. Pelham in a genuine liking for the two
Yorkshiremen. Following a brief stay at Newport, the Harrisons
cleared outwards for Cape Fear on June 6, luckily escaping a
visitation of the smallpox. "And on Peter's Leaving us, being
bound for the Carolinas," the condescending merchant remembered, "I gave him a Cask of Rum to begin in the world. At this
time he hadn't a Shilling and his Mother, Supported on Charity,
Consequently not in a Capacity of doing anything for him." Poor
or rich, base- or well-born, the brothers were personable. Although Quakers, they had about them the dash and manner of
gentlemen, and after they had put to sea, the Pelhams, missing
their cheerful company, instructed John Banister to write Joseph
that they "return your kind remembrance." [14]

13. Banister to Lee, Jan. 13, 1748/9, Banister Letter Book, 1748.
14. Pelham Family Tree, Van Buren Papers; John L. Sibley, *Biographical
Sketches of Those Who Attended Harvard College* (Cambridge, 1881), II, 416-20;
Joseph Harrison to Sir Grey Cooper, Audit Office, Loyalist Series, Bundle 68,
Public Record Office, London, cited hereafter as A. O.; Banister to J. Harrison,
Dec. 7, 1739, Banister Letter Book, 1739.

The *Sheffield's* run to Cape Fear proved most wearing, for this was the hurricane season, and the waters off Hatteras are proverbially rough. Writing to Captain Harrison in October, John Banister said he was "heartily concern'd you have mett with so much Fatigue, but a successful voyage will make up for it and [I] hope give your Owners that satisfaction as to Countenance your Bro. in the Command of your Ship. Otherways I shall endeavour to make some provision for him." [15] Joseph Harrison was about to enter Banister's employ and in this letter we glimpse for the first time the elder brother's lifelong solicitude for Peter's welfare and determination to help him along in the world.

Although it is evident that by the fall of 1739 Peter Harrison possessed sufficient experience to warrant a ship of his own, he failed to get his brother's vessel and returned to Newport in search of a job. Banister "immediately gave him the Command of a Ship, . . ." and "Sent him home with Such Recommendations to his Princaple owner that he directed me to Sett up a Learger vessell, about 300 Tons. And this Mr. Peter came over to Command her." [16] That a great London merchant, Joseph Leathley of Cheapside, should have selected this young Yorkshireman as master of one of the largest ships in the American trade was proof that virtually overnight he had risen to the top of his trade. To receive command of a vessel at twenty-three occasioned no comment in those days; mere striplings often strode the quarter deck.

Toward the end of August, 1740, "Captain Peter Harrison" returned from London to Newport as a passenger with Captain Patterson bearing instructions from Joseph Leathley to assume

15. Banister to J. Harrison, Oct. 8, 1739, *ibid*.

16. The capricious spelling and weird syntax of John Banister's letters are not altogether his fault. All quotations are taken from his letter books, which were commonly kept by an apprentice. Throughout I have made slight changes in punctuation and capitalization in the interests of clarity. Banister to Thomas Lee, Jan. 13, 1748/9, Banister Letter Book, 1748.

command of a vessel John Banister was building for him. Banister immediately sent Harrison to Providence with a letter of introduction to Benjamin Darling, owner of the yard where the hull of the ship *Leathley* rested on the ways. "You'l oblige me," wrote the merchant, "to follow his Directions in all respects concerning her. Allso the Carver. Capt. Harrison you'l find to be an Ingeneous young comander in regard to finishing and adorning a vessell." [17]

Methodically and intelligently Peter Harrison went about superintending the launching and fitting of the *Leathley*. "Sundry Accompts" in the Banister cash books and ledgers concerning this vessel, "Built in Providence by Benjamin Darling, Furnished here by me, Peter Harrison, Commander," graphically portray to landlubbers of another age the almost baffling complexity of fitting, rigging, and furnishing a large sailing ship in the eighteenth century and indicate in minute detail that such an undertaking gave work to virtually everyone at Newport. [18]

Up to the time of launching, as we have seen, Harrison dealt chiefly with the shipwrights at Providence. After Nathaniel Toogood towed the *Leathley* down Narrangansett Bay and made her fast alongside Pelham's Wharf at Newport, a swarm of artisans and craftsmen boarded her and by applying their arts and skills rapidly transformed the stark hull into a thing of grace and beauty —a noble three-masted, square-rigged ship, carrying a spanker on the mizzen as well. It was these men—smiths, founders, blockmakers, joiners, carvers, ship chandlers, painters, sailmakers, riggers, tanners, tallow chandlers, coopers, glaziers—whom youthful Peter Harrison supervised in the completion of the vessel. All the while supplies kept arriving, and wharfage had to be arranged

17. Banister to P. Harrison, to Carpenter, to Darling, and to Eagleston, Sept. 4, 1740, Banister Letter Book, 1739.

18. *Ibid.*, p. 114; Banister Account Book, 1739-44, pp. 48-50, 97, 190, 211, 212, and especially 241-44, Newport Historical Society.

for the cargo; finally Benjamin King, the instrument-maker, came over the side to set the compass in the binnacle and deliver his newly-made quadrant, glasses, and other navigating gear to the master, who would depend on his own skill and their accuracy to take the new craft safely across the ocean.

By early December puffing Negro laborers were busy loading and stowing cargo in the hold of the *Leathley*. The largest and heaviest item was logwood from the Mosquito Coast valued at £1452.1.8, but the most arresting was a parcel of twenty-two elephant teeth from Africa consigned to "Mr. Edward Pelham, merchant," in London. That much was expected of the master of a ship in these perilous times of war is indicated by the sailing orders Banister issued on November 24:

Capt. Peter Harrison

You having command under God of the ship Leathly now lying in the Harbour of Newport, Laden and ready to sail, my orders are that you improve the first convenient opportunity and proceede for London either through the English channel or North [Sea], leaving it to your Discression, and please God you arrive at your intended Port. Apply to your owner Mr. Joseph Leathly (at the Ring in Laurence Lane, Cheepside, London) and follow his direction for your future proceedings, Having a regard to the Delivery of your Cargoe according to Bill of Laden. But in case you should be taken by the French in the prosecution of your voyage (which God forbid) Transmit [to] your owner, allso Mr. John Thomlinson (to whome the great part of your Cargoe is consigned) the necessary proofs in order for their recovering the insurance, and in case you should be taken as aforesaid I give you liberty to draw on my Credit upon the above mentioned Capt. John Thomlinson for twenty pounds ster. I wish you a prosperous voyage and happy sight of your owner and friends in England.

To these orders was added a postscript, ironically more applicable to the trader, who was a notorious smuggler, than to the mariner, enjoining Captain Harrison to conduct himself at all times with circumspection: "Be sure to speak with no vessel on your passage nor suffer any to speak with you, if you can possibly avoid it; be sure [to] run no risque of loosing your ship for want of Pilots; keepe good orders on board, and by no means braking Acts of Trade." In Banister's receipt book the mariner wrote: "With Gods permission I promise to follow" these orders.[19]

Despite grave threats to shipping from Spanish privateers, the great ship dropped down the harbor on the fifth of December and stood out to sea. Two days later, in a letter to Mr. Leathley, Banister reported Harrison's sailing, and added, "I have agreed he be paid 14 £ sterl. upon his arrival in London, over and above the six pounds per month" salary. Thoughts of the new ship aroused the Rhode Islander's pride as he assured Leathley that "your vessell is as fine a Boat as ever was built in this Country." [20]

War and its consequences dictated the course of the brothers' lives for nearly two decades after they arrived at Newport in 1739. By the next year Joseph had permanently entered Banister's employ and, as a trusted agent, assisted him in countless ways to adjust to emergency conditions as the War of Jenkins' Ear expanded into King George's War (1739-1748) and exposed colonial shipping to attack by the French as well as the Spanish. Using London connections, he worked out a lucrative traffic in rice and naval stores with George Burrington and Edward Moseley in the newly-developed Cape Fear region of North Carolina and also a promising trade with several of the leading merchants at Charles Town in South Carolina. Crossing to England in 1743, he arranged with his friend Christopher Scott to open a direct commerce with Hull and Liverpool, and also through Scott procured orders for the construction of several slavers from the great Liverpool trader,

19. Banister to Peter Harrison, Nov. 24, 1740, Banister Letter Book, 1739, pp. 114, 132.
20. Banister to J. Leathley, Sept. 19, Dec. 7, 1740, *ibid.*

Joseph Manesty. At this time also, Harrison was appointed American agent for Foster, Cunliffe and Company of London. During Banister's protracted visits to England Joseph managed the merchant's affairs under a power of attorney. In addition, he supervised the building of several ships, took shares for his employer in numerous precarious but profitable privateering ventures, and successfully sought out markets in New Hampshire, Massachusetts, and the Carolinas for the European goods imported by the House of Banister.[21]

For Joseph Harrison the transition from sea to shore, from quarter deck to counting house, was complete when he was made a freeman of Rhode Island in 1745. Throughout the continental colonies he had built up a wide circle of important and influential friends. At Portsmouth they referred to him as "the Rhode Island Engineer." In view of his experience, knowledge of trade, and success in commerce it was not surprising that Joseph Harrison should aspire to a mercantile business of his own.[22]

Slowness of trade and the uncertainties caused by war and weather, the very conditions that enabled Joseph to lay the foundations of the family reputation at Newport, conspired to impede the advancement of his sea-faring brother. Captain Peter Harrison took the *Leathley* safely to London toward the end of February, 1741, fully expecting to sail promptly for North Carolina with a cargo Mr. Leathley was to have assembled and ready for him, but unforeseen difficulties and dangers on the high seas delayed

21. Joseph Harrison's services to John Banister may be traced in the latter's Letter Books and Invoice Book at the Newport Historical Society, and in Rhode Island Land Records, V, 219-20, 492-94, R. I. Archives. For the young man's reputation, see *Bowdoin and Temple Papers*, I, 72, in Massachusetts Historical Society, *Collections*, 6th ser., 9 (1897), hereafter cited as *Bowdoin and Temple Papers*.

22. J. R. Bartlett, ed., *Records of the Colony of Rhode Island and Providence Plantations* (Providence, 1857-65), V, 109, hereafter cited as *R. I. Col. Recs.*

FIGURE 2. Wyeston Hall, Bawtry in Nottinghamshire, the seat of Jonathan Acklam, where Peter and Joseph Harrison visited as boys. *From Gill and Guilford, The Rector's Book of Clayworth, Notts.*

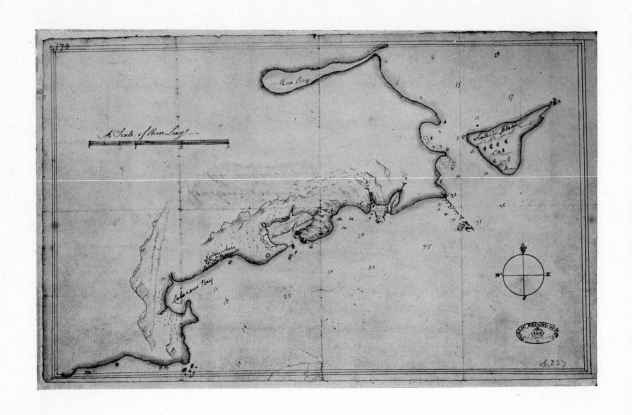

FIGURE 3. Peter Harrison's first known drawing, a plan of Louisburg and vicinity, 1745. *Public Record Office, London*

his departure until June. Rapidly picking up rice and naval stores along the Cape Fear River, he headed the *Leathley* directly back to London in mid-September, utilizing the Gulf Stream with a skill principally known to Rhode Islanders in order to make the quickest possible voyage. So hazardous was the Atlantic crossing at this time that one of his passengers, canny James Murray of Wilmington, had himself insured for £500 sterling "that we may have Some Money to Spend Among the Spaniards in Case we are Nabb'd by them." [23]

Not until the following spring did Captain Harrison make another voyage with the *Leathley*. When he reached Charles Town sometime in May, 1742, with a cargo of European goods he immediately sent off a letter to John Banister reporting his safe arrival with the sailcloth and cordage the Newporter was anxiously awaiting. Upon receipt of the letter on June 3 the merchant immediately replied advising the master not to ship any more hands and concluded mysteriously: "Ant time to enlearge," but "shd be glad to see you soone at Rhd. Island, being . . . Needfull." [24]

At Charles Town, meanwhile, Peter Harrison discharged his cargo and made arrangements for another to carry to England by way of Rhode Island. In so doing he gained the friendship of several of the most eminent merchants of the Southern port, particularly Gabriel Manigault, who entertained him at his house several times and treated him "with much Civility." [25] Not until late in September or early in October did the *Leathley* make Newport Harbor with a consignment of coats, shirts, and other cloth-

23. Years later the mariner and the merchant would be fellow officers of the Royal Customs in New England. Smithsonian Institution, *Report*, 1929 (Washington, 1930), 286; N. M. Tiffany, ed., *Letters of James Murray, Loyalist* (Boston, 1901), 50.

24. Banister to Leathley, July 15, Aug. 23, Nov. 19, 1741; May 22, 1742; to P. Harrison, June 3, 1742, Banister Letter Book, 1739.

25. Peter to Elizabeth Harrison, Charles Town, Mar. 23, 1747, Van Buren Papers.

ing which her master had purchased in London for Mr. Banister at a cost of £241.18.0.[26]

Upon coming ashore Peter Harrison learned to his amazement that he was a leading figure in the most important lawsuit then pending in the Rhode Island courts. It all came about this way. Edward Pelham, who died in 1740, made provision in his will for his widow, Arabella, and left property worth £20,000 sterling to each of his daughters—Hermione, Elizabeth, and Penelope. John Bennett and John Banister, husband of Hermione, were named executors, and Nicholas Easton, yeoman, was appointed guardian of Elizabeth, who was twenty years old and unmarried.[27] Handsome though this estate was, it resembled so many colonial legacies in that there was insufficient cash with which to settle Edward Pelham's outstanding debts, and the estate was entailed.

Shortly after the will was probated, John and Hermione Banister, Elizabeth Pelham, and Penelope Cowley took steps to dock the entail. Part of the legal legerdemain necessary to break the entails was a series of fictitious suits for common recovery. Since Joseph Harrison, upon whom he usually relied in personal and confidential matters, had been stricken by malaria at Cape Fear, John Banister interposed Peter as the party of the third part so necessary in the fictitious transfers, and on June 28, 1742, had the Pelham estate transferred to Peter with the right to sue out a writ of entry before the last day of the September court session.[28]

26. Banister Invoice Book, 1739, p. 131.

27. The will is printed in Charles T. Brooks, *The Controversy Touching the Old Stone Mill in the Town of Newport, Rhode Island* (Newport, 1851), 85-88. On November 5, 1741, Penelope Pelham had married Joseph Cowley of Wolverhampton, England, and New York. He was a merchant and was admitted as a freeman of Rhode Island on May 4, 1742. *Boston Evening Post*, Nov. 23, 1741; *R. I. Col. Recs.*, V, 42.

28. Petitions to the General Assembly, IV, 165; R. I. Land Records, V, 21-22; Fines and Recoveries, 1727-50, pp. 253, 255-57, 260-61, 273-88; Cases in Equity, 1742, IV, 25, nos. 1, 2, R. I. Archives.

Small wonder that Banister regarded Peter's presence at Newport as "being Needfull." When the sea captain appeared in person on November 24, the court ordered that there be restored to him the houses and lands "which the said Peter Harrison claims as Right and Inheritance"—that is, for the purposes of these suits. Shortly thereafter the litigation ceased, the entails were broken and each of the three daughters enjoyed full possession of her share of the estate in fee simple.[29]

Relieved by the successful termination of the long legal action, Banister was eager to be off to England on business. Peter Harrison had made his last voyage in command of the *Leathley* and was committed to take over a brig owned by a "Mr. Bluysdeens," a Holland merchant, but Banister procured his release, and wrote to John Thomlinson, owner of the ship *Triton*, that when Captain Bonfield arrived with that vessel he would offer Peter Harrison "the command of the Ship if he inclines."[30]

Captain Harrison apparently sailed for England in the summer of 1743, and for the next two years we can find no trace of him. He was now in Banister's employ, and, considering the very dangerous conditions on the high seas, it may be assumed that the *Triton* was not sent out during this period.[31] War was playing its usual havoc with maritime traffic.

The easy access from the sea to an excellent harbor that accounted for Newport's greatness in peaceful times rendered it unusually vulnerable in time of war. After 1744 fear of French privateers, especially the redoubtable Captain Murphy, alias Mor-

29. Fines and Recoveries, 1727-50, pp. 259-60.
30. Banister Letter Book, 1739, pp. 264, 267.
31. In 1747 Banister hinted at this when he was trying to blacken the captain's character by calling Peter "an idle lazy chap that has made but one voyage in six years." We know of two definitely, and have some evidence of a third before 1745. Banister to Scott, June 7, 1747, Banister Letter Book, 1748.

pang, prodded the Rhode Island Assembly into bestirring itself about fitting the crumbling works at Fort George, opposite the town on Goat Island, for defense. When the Lords of Trade and Plantations were petitioned to provide an adequate supply of cannon and military stores for the fort, reply was made that the Board of Ordnance could make no decision about the kind of cannon to send until a "Plan or Profile of the Fort" certified by the governor and "Surveyor" came over. Considering the crisis, the justifiable alarm of the Rhode Islanders, and the late hour, one would expect to learn that plans were rushed immediately to London; yet none reached the Board of Ordnance until October, 1746! [32]

Various factors produced this unwarrantable delay of two years. Not until May, 1745, did the General Assembly appoint a committee to "procure a draught or plan, of Fort George and the Harbour of Newport, in order to be sent home." [33] Their choice of a person to perform this service was naturally Peter Harrison, whose knowledge of surveying, construction, character of the harbor, and skill in drafting were capped by a known interest in fortifications. He was not available in May, however, because he was up at Portsmouth performing a service of even greater import.

A French privateer, probably commanded by Captain Morpang, had captured Peter Harrison's ship in April or May and taken her into Louisburg as a prize. There the crews of this and other English vessels were imprisoned. Although a prisoner, the Rhode Island master somehow managed to acquire an accurate knowledge of the coast, harbor, and navigational hazards of Cape Breton, and the state of the defenses at Louisburg. When he was returned to New England under a flag of truce, he placed his infor-

32. Kimball, *Correspondence*, I, 280, 308, 311, 314, 342, 433; II, 2, 3*n*.; *R. I. Col. Recs.*, V, 189-90.
33. *R. I. Col. Recs.*, V, 117.

mation at the disposal of his New Hampshire friends who were planning William Pepperell's expedition to take "the Dunkirk of America." When Governor Shirley of Massachusetts wrote to the Duke of Newcastle on November 9, 1744, about the projected attack he enclosed "an accurate plan of the harbour of Louisburg at Cape Breton taken by one Captain Harrison while a prisoner there as also a good plan of the island of Cape Breton and gut of Canso." [34]

In the Public Record Office at London there is a manuscript map which is here reproduced (Figure 3) because it is the earliest existing specimen of Peter Harrison's drawing. Although it bears evidence of hasty preparation, the map is accurately drawn and gives essential information such as soundings, islands, and reefs, as well as the height of land behind the fortress. It is likely that this map was prepared at the request of Harrison's friend, Governor Benning Wentworth, who at this time looked upon himself as the probable commander of New England's great crusade, but, regardless of that fact, the Newporter's plan of Cape Breton "facilitated its capture in the war." [35]

Upon his return to Newport, Captain Harrison regaled his fellow-townsmen with a vivid description of Cape Breton and his experiences there, which one of them communicated to the press.

34. Shirley to Newcastle, Nov. 9, 1744, C. O. 5: 900, p. 135, quoted by George A. Wood, *William Shirley* (New York, 1920), 236; Charles H. Lincoln, ed., *The Correspondence of William Shirley* (New York, 1912), I, 132, 145, 147, 148, 151-52, 161.

35. The ink wash covering the coast line appears to have been added by another hand. Comparison of this map with "A Plan of the Town and Harbour of Newport on Rhode Island" (Figure 11), made in 1755, reveals an identity in the style of the soundings figures. Some idea of the difficulty in procuring good maps in colonial cities may be had from a description of Louisburg in the *New York Post-Boy* of June 17, 1745, which was illustrated by a crude wooden map, "rough as it is, for want of good Engravers here." Joseph Harrison described his brother's map and its value in the campaign in a letter to Sir Grey Cooper of the Treasury in 1784. A. O.: Bundle 68.

He found the inhabitants and garrison weak, "and Fortifications in an ill state." All shipping was laid up except the fishing fleet, which was out on the Grand Banks. The French naval force consisted of only two poorly-armed sloops and Captain Morpang's schooner—"a poor weak Vessel." (In the light of his recent experience with Morpang, this aside appears gratuitous.) The ration for prisoners was restricted to a pound of unbaked bread and a piece of fish per day—"but no Meat!" Harrison stoutly maintained he "did not taste a Morsel while he was there." The lower room of the gaol was "half Leg deep in Nastiness," although the prisoners did sleep on dry boards in another chamber—"but no Bed!" The crowning humiliation, however, was the fact that all were forced to endure "worse treatment from some Creatures in the Shape of Englishmen than from the French themselves." [36]

The Committee of the Rhode Island Assembly seems to have approached Joseph Harrison, himself a surveyor, about preparing plans for Fort George, and he, in turn, seems to have referred them to his brother, for at colony expense, John Peckham made "a bord for Mr. Harsen to plas the Draught of the Harbour on." First, however, Peter, Joseph, and the committee went over to Goat Island to view the works, talk with the gunner, inspect the equipment, and make careful surveys of Fort George and the harbor. This expedition was something like a military inspection with a parading of the garrison and entertainment for all hands. On September 23 the gunner submitted a bill for £6.16.0 disbursed for seventeen quarts of rum consumed during the survey. This was served to the troops only, for the next day George Wanton sent in his expense account for entertaining the committee:

36. Although this account cannot be definitely ascribed to Peter Harrison, internal evidence strongly suggests his authorship. *Pennsylvania Gazette*, July 19, 1744.

> Colony of Rhode Island
> To George Wanton
> 5 gal. Wine 28/gal.   7.0.0
> 4 days Service
>   in taken ye Survey   4.0.0
>   ─────
>   11.0.0

Rum for the men, wine for the gentlemen.

Initiated under such auspicious conditions the plans were completed by the end of September and the legislators instructed Governor Gideon Wanton to send for "Messrs. Jos. Harrison and Peter Harrison, who have presented this Assembly with a handsome Draught of Fort George, and the Harbour of Newport, very ingeniously drawn, and give them the Thanks of this Assembly for the same *since they ask no other Reward*." [37] One month later, the General Assembly requested another plan of the fort and harbor, "exactly as the same now are," and ordered the Governor to send it home "with the plan already drawn, in order to show the present circumstance, . . . as well as what alterations is proposed." The fort committee was directed to procure a piece of plate, to the value of £75, and to "present the same to Mr. Peter Harrison for his trouble in surveying and making a draught of the said fort and harbour." Buying a piece of plate was evidently more "trouble" than the committee desired to take, for at the end of the year 1745, the General Treasurer merely recorded paying "Harrison, Peter, pr. Josias Lyndon £75.0.0." [38]

Why Rhode Island authorities failed to forward the plans to England is not known, but the delay came to an abrupt end as terrifying news of the sailing of the Duc d'Anville's fleet arrived

37. The phrase in italics does not appear in the printed *R. I. Col. Recs.*, V, 131; I have used the manuscript Acts and Resolves, 1744-66, p. 113. See also, Kimball, *Correspondence*, I, 351; and French Wars, Fort George (accounts for construction), 14-15, R. I. Archives.

38. *R. I. Col. Recs.*, V, 153; General Treasury Accounts, Day-Book, 1745-1757, under date of 1745, R. I. Archives.

in mid-September and French invasion again seemed imminent. The alarmed inhabitants of Newport, gathered at a special "Council of War" on September 21-22, elected a committee of fourteen prominent citizens, including Joseph and Peter Harrison, to decide "what is proper to be done for the defence of the Government," and temporarily to "do what they think good for the Safety of the Colony." Eight days later when the General Assembly met and appropriated funds for completing the new works and altering the old battery at Fort George, responsibility for the undertaking was placed in the Newport committee, but it was Peter who superintended construction after his new plans. He also, at the request of the colony, drew a third set of plans to be sent to England.[39] In this period of a little more than a year, Captain Peter Harrison had employed his talents in rendering important service in the war effort both to his community and to the colonies as a whole.

War conditions and demands for public service served to keep Peter Harrison ashore in 1745 and 1746, and, as usual, he lodged with the family of James Gould, who was also master of a Banister vessel. Such a respite would seem well-earned by one who had spent some time in a French prison. His first need was a new outfit of clothes, and he purchased at Banister's store such items as a pair of boots costing £4 and two dozen "silk becant buttons" for £5.10.0. Curiously enough, he also acquired a tea kettle, a pair of sad irons, 2 pint decanters, 3 tea pots, 2 cream pitchers, 2 "Juglets and Basons," saucers, plates, 2 "black drink Horns,"

39. Because none of these early plans could be located at the Public Record Office or other London repositories, consideration of Peter Harrison's skill as a military engineer will be deferred until his next venture in the construction of fortifications on Goat Island. Newport Town Meeting Records, II, 44, Newport Historical Society; *R. I. Col. Recs.*, V, 189-90; Letters from the Governor, I, 65; Reports and Petitions to the Rhode Island General Assembly, I, 135, 137, R. I. Archives.

and other articles scarcely needed by a bachelor who lived in one room.[40]

When he had first called at the Pelham mansion back in 1739, Peter Harrison could not have been blind to the charms of Mistress Elizabeth, and on succeeding visits he had come to know her better, especially during the maneuvers for breaking the entails on her estate in 1742.[41] That Elizabeth Pelham and Peter fell in love should occasion no surprise. Combining, as the colonial press would have put it, "great Beauty, Merit and Charm," this twenty-one-year-old "Spinster" possessed, in addition, Leamington Farm and other property worth £20,000, and enjoyed an unrivalled social position—"qualities certain to insure Success in the Conjugal State." (Figure 5) To say that Peter Harrison did not find the property and social prestige of a Pelham connection almost as attractive as its possessor would be to belie his own ambition and the prevailing attitude of his century. Marriage to Elizabeth would raise Peter to the highest plane of colonial society. It would make him a gentleman.

Nor was Peter a bad match! His Quakerism was fast dissolving under the proselyting Episcopalian pressure of his friends and his natural inclination for the formality of the Anglican service as well as the distinction attaching to its communicants. Young, handsome, cultured, successful, widely-traveled, and an Englishman, he seemed to Elizabeth an ideal suitor. (Figure 4)

Sometime after June, 1743, when Elizabeth had come of age and the entail of her share of the Pelham estate had been docked, the couple began to talk of marriage. There were, as one might

40. Banister Waste Book, 1744-46, pp. 646, 648, 680, 685, 729, 845, 847, 848, 920, Newport Historical Society; Katherine Gould's Deposition, 1822, Van Buren Papers; R. I. Land Records, V, 443-44.

41. Hermione Pelham was born on December 3, 1718; Elizabeth on October 20, 1721; Penelope on May 23, 1724. James N. Arnold, *Vital Records of Rhode Island* (Providence, 1891-1901), IV, 109.

expect, family objections, most loudly voiced by John Banister; so Elizabeth and Peter bided their time. Had the merchant been more alert, however, he would have noticed on his books that Elizabeth's slave, Jupiter, was making increasingly frequent visits to his store to purchase silks and linens for a trousseau, besides china and "various sundries" for her anticipated household.[42]

In the midst of his work on the fortifications after his return from captivity in 1745, Peter Harrison seized the opportunity to renew his courtship of Elizabeth Pelham. His devotion was ardently returned, but when the couple again made known their desire to wed, the Banisters and Pelhams objected strenuously to Peter, telling Elizabeth the age-old story that although "his character was irreproachable," nevertheless, "the family did not consider it a match her rank entitled her to." [43] This, of course, was true. The youthful sea captain could not point to a kinsman as distinguished as the Duke of Newcastle, nor to an aunt as genteel as John Banister's "My Lady Say and Sele!" Considering her wealth, social position, and beauty, the family believed that Elizabeth could make a far better match than marriage with this penniless sea-going nobody who, her brother-in-law insisted, was merely "pushing for a fortune." [44]

This denial of their desires proved a bitter disappointment to the two young people, who were actually very much in love. Their passion for each other in no way diminished; in fact, ardor overcame discretion, and early in the winter of 1746 Elizabeth Pelham found herself with child. When the couple immediately "ran away" to New Hampshire where Peter had many sympathetic friends, John Banister was in London, and no one at Newport expressed surprise at what they took to be an ordinary—and

42. Banister Account Book, 1747, pp. 114-15.
43. Affadavit of Elizabeth Brenton, 1822, Van Buren Papers.
44. Banister to Scott, June 4, 1747, Banister Letter Book, 1748.

expected—elopement. Procuring a marriage license at Portsmouth from his friend Governor Benning Wentworth, Peter took Elizabeth to the George Tavern at near-by Hampton Falls. The Quaker and the Anglican were joined in marriage by the Reverend Joseph Whipple, Congregational minister, who entered in the church records:

> 1746 June 6 married
> Mr. Peter Harrison &   Road
> Mrs. Elisabeth Pelham   Island
> L[icensed] Gov. Wint.[45]

In the nineteenth century, when Peter's descendants sought proof of the ceremony for evidence in an English lawsuit, no person then living at Newport expressed any doubts at all. So circumspect were the movements of Peter and Elizabeth and so tight-lipped were their Portsmouth abettors that few persons in Newport ever doubted his statement on his return that he had been married.

Towards midsummer the newly-weds took up their residence at Newport. As Captain Gould's daughter, Katherine, recalled the circumstances, their lodger "went into the country and was absent for some time, and when he returned he told our father and mother that he would introduce to them in his wife, and he accordingly introduced to them and us Elizabeth Pelham as his wife." That summer the Harrisons lived with the Goulds, who were Quakers, and it was probably at their house that Elizabeth gave birth to a daughter, who was baptised Hermione after her aunt Mrs. Banister on September 21, 1746.[46]

What a sensation of supreme satisfaction must have been Peter's when he refused to produce proofs of his marriage for John Banister upon his return from England in December! The merchant's

45. Hampton Falls Church Records, 88, New Hampshire Historical Society.
46. The date of birth would have been a day or so prior to the baptism. Arnold, *Vital Records of Rhode Island*, X, 504.

anger knew no bounds. Desiring to discredit both Peter and his brother with English merchants, since he was forced "to make the best of a bad market" at Newport, he wrote Christopher Scott a vicious and highly-colored description of the birth of his niece:

In a word when I came home I found everything in the utmost confusion. Goods in the store wrong mark'd, no cash enter'd in the books since July, . . . which I partly attribute to a scandalous affair of Peter Harrison, who finally got Betty Pelham with child and was so foolish as to bring a Doctor up from Boston twice, at the expense of £100, to cure Mrs. Betty (as he said, of the Hystericks). He [the physician] directly said she was near her time. Peter denyd, saying she was as chast as Lucretia, that he did not know whether she was a man or a woman, and she to the last denying his ever knowing her. But before the Doctore left the chamber Mrs. Betty's Hysteriks miraculously produced a thumping Daughter with the doctor's assistance, no body else present. Then this Ridiculous Peter went into the street. 'Gentlemen, why don't you wish me joy?' 'At what?' 'Why, I am marryd and have a daughter, etc.' All I desrd when I came home was to be satisfied they were married and I should be content, tho it were after the child was born. J. H. told me his Brother thot nobody had a right to inquire.[47]

47. Banister to Scott, Dec. 21, 1746, Banister Letter Book, 1748. Three years later the irate Rhode Islander told a different story to a London correspondent:
"Some time after he [Peter] Emparqued, I went off to London. In my absence he was taken and Returned and finally had the Impudence to take Sanctuary at my house, where he got acquainted with Mrs. Banister's Sister, now for what I know his [blank]. Let that be as it will, time Shew'd he'd been to free with the Unhappy Orphin, and in order to distroy the Effects of his Baseness Persuaded her to take Such Draughts as brought her very near her end. And in short, a Compleater Scene of Folley and Roguery never was Complicated. And on my coming home, you'l of Course Conclude me under great Confusion by having my family so Treated by a beggarly Rascall who I had Introduc'd. However, I was determin'd to make the best of a bad markett. Accordingly, I wrote him a Letter and Told him I would over Look all provided he would satisfy me of his marriage. The Dog, with his Demure face, answer'd by Letter that [he] had Refused Satisfying others and wondered I should expect it. And thus the matter at this day stands." The palpable falsehood in the last sentence gives the lie to the rest of the account, as the following pages will show. Banister to Thomas Lee, Jan. 13, 1748/9, Banister Letter Book, 1748.

That Peter Harrison summoned the best medical assistance New England afforded is not to be doubted, nor is his pride in the birth of a daughter he fondly called "Miny" to be questioned. Mr. Scott was not credulous enough to accept Banister's confessedly hearsay account of the scene with the doctor. In the course of time there were other offspring, and, as one social arbiter of the town later argued, the Harrison children "were so well received in Society and so universally respected" that there could have been no local gossip about their parents. Whatever happened was kept in the family. A rare accomplishment this, for a small town! [48]

What, then, was John Banister's motive in gratuitously slandering the good name of Peter Harrison by branding him at one and the same time an ingrate, a double-crosser, a seducer, an abortionist, and a lying knave? That Peter had married above his station was indeed true. Moreover, Edward Pelham had left Elizabeth an estate of £20,000 sterling and as one of the executors under the will John Banister controlled this property.[49] According to the law, management of the estate would pass to Peter, as Elizabeth's husband, and the erstwhile employee would become independent of the merchant, possibly even a competitor.

Banister had assured the latter eventuality when he landed at Portsmouth on November 25, 1746, escorting Eleanor Ridgway, niece of Jonathan Acklam of Bawtry, who had come over to marry Joseph Harrison.[50] The bridegroom met them at the dock

48. Miss Brenton's Supplementary Affadavit, Van Buren Papers.
49. Brooks, *The Controversy Touching the Old Stone Mill*, 85-88.
50. Eleanor Ridgway descended from the Acklams of Yorkshire through her mother, Anna, who was the sister of Jonathan Acklam of Wyeston in Nottinghamshire. When her mother died, Eleanor went to live as a ward of her Uncle Jonathan, and in 1743 was acting as housekeeper for Wyeston in the customary manner of sisters or nieces in eighteenth-century English county families. From Wyeston on September 27, Joseph Harrison wrote to his principal reporting success with his courtship: "The only difficulty is with her Uncle, who (tho my very good friend) will never be prevailed on to give her a suitable fortune till I am fixed in some settled way of business. I doubt not that you may be very

and the ceremony was performed that very night in Queen's Chapel.[51] At this time, and in the presence of his bride, the merchant charged Joseph with neglect and "unparalleled folley" in the handling of affairs during his absence, and announced his intention "to have intirely done" with the young man. He paid dearly for this egregious blunder by making an implacable enemy of Eleanor Ridgway Harrison. "That smart Dame" of Joseph's succeeded in making more trouble than the merchant had ever dreamed of. "What course his Lady will next direct," he commented sourly some months later, "I know not." About all that was left was to accuse Peter, "an idle lazy chap," of leading Joseph astray—even to drink! [52]

After such experiences the brothers resolved to free themselves from Banister's bullying and domineering management. They no longer needed his guidance. Towards the close of 1746 they left his employ, formed a partnership of their own, and proceeded immediately to seek out trade. As one would expect, the elder brother remained at Newport to conduct the business from the counting house, while the younger brother set out on the nautical road to traffic for goods, freights, and commissions. John Banister's almost hysterical attempts to blacken their names failed dismally.[53] To most Rhode Island merchants as they reviewed the experience

serviceable in bringing about the affair when you come to England." Three years later, despite advice to the contrary from Christopher Scott, Banister persuaded "Miss Nelly" to cross to New Hampshire in the mast ship. Joseph Harrison to Banister, Hull, June 14, July 30, 1746; Banister to Scott, Newport, Dec. 21, 1746, Banister Letter Book, 1748.

51. Parish Register of Queen's Chapel, Portsmouth, N. H., typescript, American Antiquarian Society.

52. Banister to Scott, Dec. 21, 1746; Apr. 9, 1746/7, June 7, 1747, Banister Letter Book, 1748.

53. War-worry and heavy losses in privateering may have contributed to set this irascible and unscrupulous man's nerves on edge. *Commerce of Rhode Island*, Massachusetts Historical Society, *Collections*, 7th ser., 9 (1914), 54-55; Manesty to Banister, Mar. 30, 1747, Banister Letter Book, 1748.

and the character of its members, the new House of Harrison appeared destined for a prosperous future.

In anticipation of a prolonged absence from home, Peter Harrison moved his little family from the Goulds' to new lodgings at the house of William Crossing.[54] Although he made every possible arrangement for the comfort of mother and child, it is clear that he felt he must succeed in business before he attempted to live in the style of the Pelhams and Banisters.

Early in 1747 he journeyed overland to Boston to assume command of a new vessel that he and Joseph acquired there through Henry Frankland, Collector of the Port, because John Banister controlled virtually all the shipbuilding in Narragansett Bay. This trip marked the beginning of travels that would keep him away from Newport for the better part of two years. Such a separation was hard on both Elizabeth and "Miny" as well as Peter. Yet it was typical of life among all sea-faring families at Newport and other colonial cities of the century. Primitive communications generally prevented Peter and Elizabeth from hearing from each other for months at a time, but in this particular case there have survived seven letters written by the youthful master to his wife.

Addressed to "my dearest Betty" or "my dearest Angel" by "My Charming Betty's Ever Constant and faithful Servt. P. Harrison," these are the letters of a young man who was very much in love. They reveal a deep concern for the health of mother and child, as well as brave attempts to ease his wife's alarm lest he once again fall into the clutches of the enemy. There are comments about business, plans for the future, places visited, and persons encountered. Written during wartime for family perusal only, they naturally deal with objects rather than ideas, although in

54. He was a brother of the well-known Dr. Thomas Crossing. Newport Town Council Records, XV, 54-55, Newport Historical Society; *Newport Mercury*, Jan. 2, 1769.

occasional references one can discern certain clues bearing on the future of the Harrisons.

Peter Harrison busied himself with domestic affairs as he waited for a thaw sufficient to allow his ship to beat her way out of Boston harbor. He solved the servant problem by persuading Mrs. Greenleaf, a relative of his friend Sheriff Stephen Greenleaf, to go to Newport in April as Mrs. Harrison's housekeeper. When "His Grace, Mr. Banister, Currlike," showed his teeth by hiring Boston's leading lawyer, "Leather-Jacket" John Read, who pioneered in the use of technicalities, to force Peter to post bonds for a small debt which Joseph had agreed to discount from a large sum Banister owed him, Peter quietly forestalled the action "by immediately paying the Old Gentleman the money." Before his departure he sent to his Betty by the post two pairs of pink worsted stockings with clocks of the same color, "which they tell me, in England is all the mode," and also assured her that the snow [55] was stout and swift: "As to my being taken by the Enemy (of which I don't apprehend much danger), but if it should happen so, . . . all the Injury it can do me, is only keeping me perhaps a month longer from England." [56]

John Banister's fears that the new mercantile house would compete with him soon came true, for Captain Peter Harrison cleared out for the Cape Fear basin early in the second week in February to solicit the business of his former employer's customers, the Honorable Edward Moseley and William Dry, collector of the port at Brunswick, North Carolina.[57] About March 16 he brought his vessel across the famous bar and dropped her anchor before Charles Town after a tedious and stormy passage. "The snow goes inimitably well," he informed Elizabeth, "otherwise we might

55. A vessel resembling a brig, carrying a main- and fore-mast as well as an auxiliary trysail-mast close abaft the main-mast.
56. Peter to Elizabeth Harrison, Boston, Feb. 2, 1746/7, Van Buren Papers.
57. R. I. Land Records, V, 572.

FIGURE 4. Peter Harrison, *ca.* 1756, by Nathaniel Smibert. *Courtesy of Maurice P. Van Buren*

FIGURE 5. Elizabeth Pelham Harrison, *ca.* 1756, by Nathaniel Smibert. *Courtesy of Maurice P. Van Buren*

have stood a chance of being taken, for there was at the time we came upon this Coast, a French Privateer Cruising at some distance from the Land and one from St. Augustine close in Shoar. The latter took no less then four Prizes in sight of the Barr that very morning we got in." [58]

After procuring lodgings suitable for a rising trader and arranging for the proper carrying-out of the ship's routine with his mate, Captain Harrison next made calls to renew his acquaintance with those "eminent merchants" whom he had met during his previous stop at the southern metropolis in 1742, or had come to know when they made summer visits to Newport. His satisfaction at being well-received and hospitably entertained and the modest pleasure he took in his social success at South Carolina are evident in his report to Mrs. Harrison:

I believe you have hear'd me speak of one Mr. Manigould,[59] who treated me the first time I was here with much Civility. He is the Treasurer of this Coloney and one of the most considerable Gentlemen in it, both for Fortune and Character. He has been since I came now, exceedingly Complaysant to me, I have Din'd and Drank Tea at his House three or four times. And as soon as he understood I was married both he and his Lady, desir'd I wou'd the first time I wrote to Rhode Island present their Compliments to you.[60]

But even tea at the Manigaults' proved a barren substitute for news from home: "As you my dearest Betty, well know the Ardent Love I have for you, which is such, that I really cannot find words to express it, You must therefore think how uneasy I am at not hearing from you." He consoled himself with purchasing

58. Peter to Elizabeth Harrison, Charles Town, Mar. 23, 1747, Van Buren Papers.

59. Gabriel Manigault, wealthiest man in South Carolina, was Treasurer of the province until 1743. Harrison was evidently not aware that the Huguenot's status had changed since his visit of 1742.

60. Peter to Elizabeth Harrison, Charles Town, Mar. 23, 1747, Van Buren Papers.

a cask of limes and oranges and a barrel of Carolina potatoes to be dispatched with his mail in Captain Bull's Newport-bound brig.[61] In a letter he counselled Betty that since Mrs. Greenleaf must have arrived by this time "you will be at liberty to go a Visiting or to Ride abroad ... I know your tender care for Miny will be a barr to those little partys of Pleasure, but I beg it may be none, for whilst the little dear Rogue's under the Care of Mrs. Greenleaf, you may be intirely easy." [62]

Charles Town was a gay place, especially at this time of the year when the planters came to town for "the Season." The harbor was active and crowded with dozens of small craft tending the seventy-odd vessels of the rice fleet, with which Peter Harrison's snow would soon sail in the company of a man o'war.[63] Amid the hustle and bustle of last minute preparations he was no doubt "agreeably distracted" by the lavish entertainments of his Carolina friends, and particularly by the opportunity to discuss his favorite topics of drawing and architecture with Gabriel Manigault, Isaac Mazyck, and other gentlemen whom he met at St. Philip's Church.

Shortly before his convoy sailed the Captain received a letter from his wife, dated March 7, which was full of disturbing news. The gentlewoman who had been reared in comfort and luxury found life in lodgings with a demanding baby and no husband lonesome, drab, and discouraging, and had poured out her troubles all at once. Mr. Crossing was exceedingly disagreeable, Miny was cutting her teeth and in addition was not very well, but worst of all the young bride feared that a persistent "Disorder" and "continual Head-ach" were causing her beauty to fade. In a last letter

61. Peter to Elizabeth Harrison, Charles Town, Mar. 28, 1747, Van Buren Papers.

62. Peter to Elizabeth Harrison, Charles Town, Mar. 23, 1747, Van Buren Papers.

63. The *South-Carolina Gazette* for December 17, 1748, lists the rice fleet of the ensuing year at seventy-three ships.

from Charles Town on April 14, the anxious husband seeks by every means to comfort his wife. He is sending more oranges and limes, and before long a vessel will arrive with the greatest of all colonial delicacies—a West India turtle—and Mrs. Harrison can then invite all of her friends to a "frolick" on Goat Island. When he returns from England with the handsome furniture they have planned for him to purchase, they will place it in the Pelham house which Elizabeth's mother has promised to make available for them. In the meantime, "I have desir'd my Brother to procure you other Lodgings, which if to be had, I intreat of you to go immediately into 'em." [64]

"You tell me in your Letter, you are much Alter'd in your Looks," he continued, "Don't let that, my Lovely Betty, make you the least uneasy, for there is no Alteration can ever vary that perfect Love I have for you, which is not to be chang'd by any accident that human life is liable to, or can deface out of my mind the Charming Appearance you made when you first promis'd to be mine." And to this endearing and soothing sentiment he added, significantly, "it won't be many months before I shall return to Rhode Island, After which you shall live in all respects to the extent of your Wishes. You well know (... it is not in my Power to deny you any thing) that it is likewise my Inclinations to appear in a handsome and genteel manner." [65]

When he reached England early in the summer of 1747, Captain Harrison set out for York in post haste to tell his mother and sisters about his wife and child. With the counting house of Christopher Scott as his base of operations, he proceeded to make business trips in all directions from Hull—to London, to Liverpool, and to Lancaster. Then there were visits to his relatives and connections at

64. Peter to Elizabeth Harrison, Charles Town, Apr. 14, 1747, Van Buren Papers.
65. *Ibid.*

Hornsea and Wyeston. It is probable, too, that on this or an earlier voyage he made a trip to Holland.

Military science, and especially the art of constructing fortifications as practiced by the great Continental masters and expounded by John Muller in England, absorbed much of the spare time of this Vauban of Narragansett Bay. Over half of his letter of September 9 from London to Elizabeth was devoted to describing in enthusiastic detail the siege of Bergen-op-Zoom by the French. "They have on both sides the most experienc'd Generals and the most expert Engineers in all Europe, who practice equally all the Stratagems that their Experience and Knowledge suggests to 'em. It is without dispute, as memorable a siege as ever was read in History, and upon the Issue of which . . . will be decided the fate of all Zealand." [66]

Peter Harrison's efforts to establish business connections and to secure credit for the new firm met with unqualified success. From London in October, 1747, he shipped to Newport a large cargo of woolens in one of John Thomlinson's ships. The following spring an even larger consignment was sent from Hull by Christopher Scott who, despite the scurrilous innuendos of John Banister, showed his faith in his protégés by granting them ample credit. Through his influence also, Peter got the business of Joseph Manesty and Company, leading slave-traders of Liverpool. Apparently Banister failed completely in his attempts to traduce the brothers; actually they seem to have risen in the esteem of English merchants when they broke with the Rhode Islander.

66. Bergen-op-Zoom, situated near the mouth of the Scheldt in North Brabant, was an elaborate "modern" fortress of just the type to intrigue Peter Harrison. He might reasonably have expected a victory when the Duke of Cumberland returned to Flanders to face Marshall Saxe, but shortly after this letter was written Cumberland retreated, permitting General Lowendal to force the capitulation of Bergen-op-Zoom and to lay siege to Maestricht. Peter to Elizabeth Harrison, London, Sept. 9, 1747, Van Buren Papers.

The decision of Scott and Manesty to trade with the Harrisons brewed Banister's groaning beer. He then turned on Scott, angrily declaring, "in a word, . . . of all insignificant Triflers you are the very pushpin of understanding. Your intended services and friendship to me I despise as I do the author." [67] Peter Harrison's trip to England had indeed borne fruit, although as early as October 22, 1747, Scott had given Banister up as a bad job and on Peter's prompting had executed a power of attorney authorizing Joseph Harrison "to ask, demand, sue for recovery and receive of and from John Banister of Newport, . . . or any other Persons indebted to me." By this act the brothers became the American agents for this leading outport merchant, who was at this time chamberlain for Hull, soon to become sheriff, and eventually lord mayor. Joseph Harrison must have read with amusement—and satisfaction—Banister's letter of the following March in which he vehemently declared his intention to have done with Christopher Scott, which was equivalent to resigning after he had been fired! [68] Such a connection greatly benefited the new firm. Within a year Scott could notify the Newport merchant Thomas Vernon: "I send Sales of the Mahogany to Messrs. Joseph and Peter Harrison." Before long the Harrisons and Vernons were enjoying a profitable trade with Thomlinson, Trecothick and Company of London, especially in marine insurance. [69]

England had its attractions for the young man, as we have seen, but he longed for his family and for Rhode Island. Surrounded by the countless stimulating diversions of London he could still

67. Peter to Elizabeth Harrison, London, Sept. 9, 1747; Apr. 3, 1748, Van Buren Papers; Banister to Leathley, Apr. 26, 1747; to Scott, July 15, 1748, Banister Letter Book, 1748.

68. Rhode Island Land Records, V, 593-94; James Cranshaw, Chief Librarian of Hull, to author, Nov. 19, 1946; Banister to J. Harrison, Mar. 17, 1747/8, Banister Letter Book, 1748.

69. Vernon Letter Books, Aug. 1743-Mar. 1777, I, 16, Newport Historical Society; Donnan, *Slave Trade*, III, 147, 168.

write to Betty: "This Absence is so tiresome that I often think, if I had the Indies, I wou'd give it with pleasure to be with you. And in short, I do assure you after my return to Rhode Island, not anything shall enduce my leaving you again." [70] He joyfully informs his wife on August 1, 1748, that in a month he will sail from Hull and should arrive in Newport by the first week in November at the latest. All the household furniture is assembled and boxed, ready for shipment. As a special surprise, "I have bought you Eighteen Yards of the richest Blue Damask I could meet with in London," he concludes. "I am advis'd not to get it made up for fear (as it cannot be exactly fitted) of its being injured in the altering." [71]

Landing in Newport after practically two years' absence, the younger Harrison scarcely had time to renew his acquaintance with his family before he was swamped with mercantile affairs. Almost immediately Judge Chambers Russell of the Court of Vice Admiralty appointed "Captain Peter Harrison . . . Merchant" to serve with his friends Thomas Vernon and William Mumford as a committee to appraise the prize snow *True Briton*.[72] The brothers' success in all their activities proved only gall and wormwood to John Banister, who had now largely given over his efforts to trade directly with England for the more lucrative Guinea Trade, and, as the war was over, for some devious, though profitable, dealings with the French and Dutch in the West Indies. He poured out his bitterness to Thomas Lee of London on January 13, 1748/9, in a self-pitying, truth-twisting letter, reviewing the history of his relations with the brothers.

Stimulating and vital as these commercial activities were, they

70. Peter to Elizabeth Harrison, London, Sept. 9, 1747, Van Buren Papers.
71. Peter to Elizabeth Harrison, London, Aug. 1, 1748, *ibid.*
72. Rhode Island Admiralty Papers, VI, 21, R. I. Archives; Dorothy B. Towle, ed., *Records of the Vice Admiralty Court of Rhode Island, 1716-52* (Washington, 1936), 489.

had to compete with two other absorbing pursuits for the young merchant's attention: the development of Leamington Farm, and the study of the gentle art of architecture in the books he had brought from England. As he contemplated the role of the gentleman, he would have agreed most heartily with the Earl of Arundel's assertion that "one who could not design a little would never make an honest man." [73] It was his ventures in design that gave historical significance to Peter Harrison's career.

73. Horace Walpole, *Anecdotes of Painting in England*, in *Works* (London, 1798), III, 207.

II

Ventures in Design

W HEN, how, and from whom Peter Harrison the mariner
acquired his training as an architect will probably never
be precisely known for lack of sufficient evidence, but it is possible
to describe in detail the milieu in which he developed his talents
and some of the factors that contributed to this development.

The year of Harrison's birth coincides with the beginning of
a new era in English architecture. For over half a century the
imaginative, unbalanced, and florid baroque style of building had
held sway, but after 1716 country lords, freshly returned from
the Grand Tour to Italy, began to react from the "half baroque"
of Sir Christopher Wren and the "whole baroque" of Sir John
Vanbrugh, Hawksmoor, and Archer. Henceforth taste became
strictly Palladian.[1]

Palladianism was a style of building, originally expressed in the
houses of English noblemen, that was destined to give form and
language to the architecture of the first half of the eighteenth
century. Like contemporary modes in painting and literature, it
took its rise from the classical tradition as reinterpreted in the six-

1. Andrea Palladio of Vicenza, after whom the Italianate movement based on
Roman inspiration took its name, was only one of several architects who influenced English building. Vitruvius, Vignola, Scamozzi, and Serlio were all partici-
pants in the "back-to-Rome" movement which so profoundly affected Inigo
Jones and others in France and England.

38

teenth century at Vicenza by Andrea Palladio, and introduced to England by Inigo Jones in the seventeenth century. The acknowledged leader of this reaction against the lingering medievalism of the seventeenth century was the Earl of Burlington, who, after a tour to Italy, gathered about himself several "architect-dependents," notably Colin Campbell, Giacomo Leoni, and William Kent. By patronage and example he succeeded in imparting an orderly and academic quality to English architecture that proved to have a lasting significance.

This was the time in England when the practice of architecture, if such it could be called, was in the hands of noblemen or in those of middle-class designers encouraged and patronized by widely-traveled nobles acquainted with Italian examples. There were no architects in the professional sense. As late as 1747, in the *London Tradesman*, R. Campbell observed: "I scarce know of any in England who have had an education regularly designed for the Profession. Bricklayers, Carpenters, etc., all commence [to be] Architects." [2] Anybody recruited from the gentlemen dilettantes, surveyors, masons, or carpenters who had the slightest association with building and design called himself an architect-carpenter. That high-born and low-born alike could do this is explained by the easy access of all to architectural books.

Books, more than any other single factor, served to establish the "dictatorship of academic taste" throughout the building world. In 1715, with the backing of the Earl of Burlington, Colin

2. The building trades of London, for example, comprised the following: 1) *Craftsmen* (carpenters, joiners, masons, plasterers, bricklayers, glaziers, plumbers, painters, carvers and paviors) who were skilled, conscientious, expensive, and who could make a good drawing; 2) *Master-Builders* (usually recruited from the ranks of the carpenters or masons); 3) *Surveyors*, who were primarily estimators of building costs; and 4) *Architects*. "But," warns John Summerson, "it cannot be too strongly emphasized that until about half-way through the 18th century there was no such thing as an 'architectural profession' in the modern sense." *Georgian London* (New York, 1946), 53-55.

Campbell published a set of superb drawings of the finest classical buildings then existing in England in the first folio volume of *Vitruvius Britannicus*. In the same year, also, Lord Burlington brought out a translation of Palladio prepared by Leoni. During the next three decades the presses issued numerous architectural works in large folios which after 1725 were accompanied literally by a flood of manuals compiled by craftsmen for their fellow-builders. From books like James Gibbs's simple though admirable *Rules for Drawing the Several Parts of Architecture* (1732) aspiring gentlemen-architects and craftsmen learned the meaning and importance of symmetry, balance, and proportion—qualities of paramount importance in classical building. Master-builders now knew for the first time how to construct a Doric, Ionic, or Corinthian column properly, what a pediment, entablature, or cornice was, and how to employ them "correctly" in building.[3] Above all, these books supplied them with acceptable models to follow and provided them with the elements of an architectural discipline. As a result, Mr. Summerson points out, "under George II Palladianism conquered not only the high places of architecture —the great patrons, the government offices—but through the medium of prints and books, the whole of the vernacular, finding its way ultimately into the workshop of the humblest carpenter and bricklayer."[4] By the 1740's Palladianism was the vogue.

In the cathedral city of York, between Peter Harrison's eighteenth and twentieth years, the famous Assembly Rooms (Figure 6) were being erected under the aegis of the Earl of Burlington, Lord Lieutenant of the shire. For anyone of the sensitive Peter's

3. Books on the orders of Vignola and Palladio had, of course, been coming from English presses for forty years before Leoni published his superb edition, but widespread dependence on such works, and the codification of proportions they represented, developed only after 1715.

4. Summerson, *Georgian London*, 21, 56, 58. For a representative collection of those works, see Peter Harrison's Inventory in Appendix C of the present work.

bent this was an undertaking of great moment. "The design was taken," a contemporary noted, "by that truly English Vitruvius, Richard, Earl of Burlington, from Palladio; who gives the plan but tells you it was never executed out of Egypt." Thus it was that at his most impressionable age the future American architect came into contact with the work of the acknowledged arbiter of English taste and patron of the Palladian manner of building. It is more than probable, too, that at this time he first met the Earl's protégé and principal assistant William Kent, who was himself a Yorkshireman. Peter was permanently influenced by the fine Palladianism of the Assembly Rooms as he observed them under construction, and to the end of his days he cherished a copy of Francis Drake's beautiful folio volume, *Eboracum, or the History and Antiquities of the City of York* (1736), which contained a detailed description and three excellent engravings of the new buildings. Dedicated to the Earl of Burlington, Drake's book was in a real sense symbolical of the role Peter Harrison would play in the American colonies.[5]

Before he went to America, Peter Harrison acquired either at York or under patronage of Christopher Scott at Hull a sound knowledge of shipbuilding and a skill in woodcarving that he never lost. Each of these crafts involved, at the least, an elementary understanding of design and some ability at draftsmanship, and the lad could have easily discovered his talent for drawing in this manner. However it was, when he went to sea he had, in addition to ship-handling, to learn the science of navigation, major features of which are plotting and the use of charts. In all these crafts Peter,

5. Drake, *Eboracum*, 337-38. On Burlington and Kent, see E. Beresford Chancellor, *Lives of the British Architects* (London, 1909), 222; B. Sprague Allen, *Tides of English Taste* (Cambridge, 1936), I, 58-60; *Dict. Nat. Biog.*, VI, 117; XXX, 23. Peter may also have taken a small-boy's interest in the old Roman camp at Pickering, near his father's birthplace. In after years Plates 6 and 9 of Drake's history served to refresh his memory of these scenes.

and also his brother Joseph, exhibited skill far above the average when they entered the service of John Banister at Newport in 1739. And they were, besides, well versed in the art of land surveying.[6]

An opportunity for further travel and a chance to improve his already considerable knowledge came to Peter when he sailed the *Leathley* for London in 1740. Conditions beyond his control kept the ship from returning to the colonies for nearly six months. Palladianism was in the air at this time and anyone with an interest in architecture could scarcely have escaped it. Through Thomlinson at London, Harrison almost certainly met William Kent again, and this devotee of Palladio would have urged him to improve his opportunities.[7] At any rate, the sea captain did not spend his time unprofitably in the manner of most mariners ashore. During his visit to England, and again in 1742, 1743, and 1744 he traveled extensively in his homeland—from London to York and Hull and to the West Country—viewing on the way many of its great architectural exhibits. He also developed a timely and permanent interest in the design and construction of fortifications, which definitely suggests familiarity with the defensive works of the Low Countries. When he came to plan Fort George in 1745 a copy of *The New Method of Fortifications, as practised by Monsieur Vauban,... made English*, recently purchased in England, provided him with the latest and most celebrated models.[8]

6. Harrison also assembled a useful collection of books on navigation and surveying. Appendix B.

7. William Kent of the North Riding became "principal painter to the Crown" in 1739. This was not his forte, however, for as William Hogarth caustically yet truthfully remarked: "neither England nor Italy ever produced a more contemptible dauber." Nor is Kent considered to have advanced the science of architecture greatly. His real contribution lay in landscape gardening. W. T. Whitely, *Artists and Their Friends in England, 1700-1799* (London, 1928), I, 34, 35.

8. See Appendix B.

Upon his return to the British Isles in 1747, he came as an established merchant who had made an unusually good marriage for a colonial. Henceforth, as he had written to Elizabeth, Peter Harrison intended to make a figure in the world and to live genteelly. With this in mind he bought English furniture of the latest fashion for the Newport house and rich fabrics for his wife and child. Smibert's portrait suggests that its subject would not overlook finery for himself.[9] To round out his preparation for his new status he again combined travel for edification and self-improvement with that for business. The letters he wrote to his wife from England indicate that he studiously widened his acquaintance with persons and places during the sojourn. Since the architectural "genius" from the North Riding was currently the rage of London, Harrison certainly once again viewed the buildings for the Horse Guards and the Treasury, as well as Devonshire House, but he seems to have been particularly impressed with Kent's fenestration at Finch House in Berkeley Square—it would turn up later in his own work.

At London, too, Harrison began the accumulation of what eventually became the largest and best-selected architectural library of colonial America. When he sailed for Newport in 1748, with all the household effects promised to his wife, he had on board a large box of books for himself. Among them was *The Designs of Inigo Jones* (1727) by William Kent, the most important architectural work of the period. Then there were other outstanding treatises sponsored by the Burlington School: Kent's *Designs for Houghton Hall, Holkham* (1736), often considered his best work; *Andrea Palladio's Architecture* (1735-36), edited by Edward Hoppus; James Gibbs's *A Book of Architecture*

9. "I intend to send you soon after I get to England, the Holland and Cambrick for my Shirts and for your own Use, with the Sheeting Linen, etc. All which I would chuse to have made up before I return." Peter to Elizabeth Harrison, Charles Town, Apr. 14, 1747, Van Buren Papers.

(1728), and his *Rules for Drawing the several Parts of Architecture* (1732). Also in the box were volumes of architectural guidance by lesser lights such as Batty Langley's recently published *The City and Country Builder's and Workman's Treasury of Designs* (1740) and the manuals of William Halfpenny, William Salmon, and John Gwynn besides other books on the arts.[10]

Given the Captain's great interest in the siege of Bergen-op-Zoom, it is not surprising that he acquired a copy of John Muller's *Treatise on the Elementary Parts of Fortifications*, first published at London in 1746. Books on new methods of farming, on family medicine, geography, and trade filled most of the chest. Yet all had not been selected solely for their practical value. Like most cultivated colonials Peter Harrison's reading tended to be serious and instructive, but occasionally he did indulge himself with a play or a book of verse, in addition to the *Gentleman's Magazine*, *Robinson Crusoe*, and a *Defense of the Female Sex*.[11]

From Portsmouth in New Hampshire to the metropolis of distant South Carolina gentlemen of capacity recognized in the thirty-three-year-old merchant a cultivated "Man of Taste," a good and willing Anglican, yet tolerant of other faiths, who through travel and by experience in making maps and building fortifications had amply demonstrated his talents. This mercantile gentry, as nascent Americans, admired him all the more because he tempered his genius with success in the world of affairs. The colonies as yet had no place for a professional architect.

But here was a rare colonial. Not a jack-of-all-trades; rather a master of *ten*—ship-handling, navigation, shipbuilding, woodcarv-

10. These books are all listed in the inventory of Peter Harrison's estate made after his death in 1775. He would have needed the works mentioned when he prepared plans for the Redwood Library, King's Chapel at Boston, and St. Michael's at Charles Town. The Batty Langley volume is not listed in the inventory. Harrison must have had access to it, or, more likely, he once owned it and had either lent it out or lost it by 1775. See Appendix C.

11. Appendix B.

ing, drafting, cartography, surveying, military engineering and construction, commerce, and the new agriculture. With the single exception of farming each of these skills contributed directly to that recognized mastery of architecture that has led some to believe he must have served an apprenticeship in England under a professional architect.[12] On the other hand, he was much more than "a cultivated amateur," for few of the English practitioners of his day who called themselves "architects" could have displayed such an impressive array of skills or such a thorough background of training for their craft. Inclination, early training, talent, and eventual status supported this artistic interest. The gradual evolution is clear. Peter Harrison was no dilettante; he was a professionally-educated architect who regarded his craft as an avocation.

In 1747, in keeping with the tradition of his forebears, one of whom founded the library at Bristol, England, in the seventeenth century, and immediately stimulated by the example of Benjamin Franklin's new Library Company at Philadelphia, Abraham Redwood gave £500 sterling for the purchase of books for a library at Newport.[13] The Company of the Redwood Library was incorporated in August, and in October, as one of the original members, Joseph Harrison was placed on a committee to collect funds for "a regular Building for a Library." The establishment of this

12. Peter Harrison's only possible family connection in the field of architecture, and this is extremely tenuous, may have been George Harrison, who advertised at Philadelphia in 1746 that he had "served an apprenticeship in London," and that he had been employed in England by several gentlemen as a "Surveyor in the designing, Making Draughts of, and Superintending their Building." He also designed chimney-pieces and all sorts of marblework. *Pennsylvania Gazette*, July 14, 1746.

13. Minute Book of the Company of the Redwood Library, 1747, pp. 1-2, in the Library, Newport, R. I.; Carl Bridenbaugh, *Cities in the Wilderness* (New York, 1938), 339-40; Carl and Jessica Bridenbaugh, *Rebels and Gentlemen* (New York, 1942), 93-94; *R. I. Col. Recs.*, V, 227.

library was one of the most important cultural developments thus far undertaken in the English colonies.

Sometime during the next nine months plans for the new structure were drawn up. Progress accelerated in June, 1748, when Henry Collins generously presented Mr. Redwood with the deed to a plot of ground adjacent to the Pelham property. At a meeting held July 4, at which Joseph Harrison was chosen a director in the place of the late Reverend John Callender, a catalogue of the books wanted was ordered to be sent promptly to John Thomlinson in London, and the Company agreed that the Directors, or any three of them, should as soon as possible "contract with such workmen as they shall please to go on and build the Library." [14] Consequently, on August 9 "Samuel Wickham, Esq., Henry Collins and John Tillinghast, Merchants," signed a contract with "Wing Spooner, Samuel Green, Thomas Melvil and Israel Chapman . . . all of Newport, . . . House Carpenters," to build the Redwood Library, "the whole to be compleated well and workmanlike according to a plan or Draught drawn by Mr. Joseph Harrison," before October 1, 1749, for the sum of £2,200 old tenor currency. [15]

The appearance of the name of Joseph Harrison in this document has baffled historians who have not previously known that Peter Harrison was in London at this juncture, and that he had for over a year been improving himself by viewing famous buildings, studying the construction of fortifications, acquiring books of architecture, and perhaps even settling the elements of taste with members of the Kent-Burlington circle. Joseph, well aware of his brother's studies and emerging reputation, apparently wrote him in the fall of 1747 soliciting a plan. Here indeed was a rare

14. Redwood Minute Book, 1-5; George C. Mason, *Annals of the Redwood Library* (Newport, 1891), 31-37.
15. This contract is printed in Appendix E.

FIGURE 6. The Assembly Rooms at York, designed by Lord Burlington with the assistance of William Kent and erected in 1735, provided the youthful Peter Harrison with an introduction to Palladian architecture. This façade is shown in Francis Drake, *Eboracum, or the History and Antiquities of the City of York.*

FIGURE 7. The Redwood Library in 1767, a watercolor drawing in the notebook of Pierre Eugène du Simitière. This is one of the very few contemporary drawings of a colonial building. *Courtesy of the Free Library of Philadelphia*

opportunity for Peter Harrison to display his "genius" at this gentleman's *métier*. He seized it. At Hornsea or Wyeston sometime before May, 1748, he must have hastily prepared preliminary designs and dispatched them to Rhode Island. They may have been merely rough sketches. In any event, to insure that they conformed with the Collins lot, which Peter knew only from memory, it became necessary for Joseph to redraw them. Although he was a competent draftsman, there is no evidence to suggest that the conception of the Redwood Library was his. Architecture was not the elder Harrison's forte.

As a director of the Redwood Library Joseph Harrison submitted plans in the development of which he served only as "man-midwife." After Peter returned and was able to view the premises and consider further the function of the building, he decided to revise his hastily-drawn plans. The modifications, which markedly enhanced the external appearance of the library and made possible the shelving of more volumes within, were embodied in a "Memorandum" of February 6, 1748/9, issued by the three directors to the house carpenters as "an Additional Agreement" providing that "in Consideration of the Builders Conforming to the sd. Draught drawn by Mr. Peter Harrison, and following his directions as to all the Alterations," they are to be paid an extra £100 old tenor.[16]

Thus, amid household and business affairs, which crowded upon Peter Harrison upon his return after two years' absence, he generously took the time to design and superintend the construction of the edifice that still houses the collections of this famous institution. In all of the continental and island colonies, be it noted, there was no building to which he could turn for an example. Colonial civil architecture was then in its infancy. Faneuil Hall and the State House at Boston, Richard Munday's Newport Colony House, the New York City Hall, and the civic buildings

16. The memorandum is printed in Appendix E.

of Philadelphia, Annapolis, and Williamsburg, which were all planned in the tradition loosely and popularly known today as "colonial" or "Georgian," held no appeal for Harrison. The carpenter-architects who built these structures followed tradition; they seldom led the fashion.

Impressed by what he had seen and studied in England, Harrison came back to Newport armed with the latest works on architecture and prepared to introduce the Palladian style to America. By returning to seventeenth-century models he became an innovator. This retrospective quality in design provides a significant parallel with current American political thinking, for colonial statesmen were beginning to seek inspiration in the republicanism of Harrington, Sidney, and Locke which was contemporary with the Palladianism of Inigo Jones—and republicanism in political theory together with classicism in architecture eventually became the mode of a new nation.

Daring to go beyond prevailing colonial types for his model for the Redwood Library, Harrison chose with unerring taste a temple-like design that had achieved considerable popularity among the English gentry. Palladio had used it in the Church of Santo Giorgio at Venice (Figure 18), while in England it had originally been employed for a garden temple by the Earl of Burlington at Chiswick (Figure 17), and by William Kent as a casino for Sir Charles Hotham, and again at Holkham in Norfolk; while at the entrance to the gardens at Stowe it was used as an eye-trap to terminate a vista. Of more importance is the fact that the design scheme was a popular one, an architectural *cliché*, and was frequently included in the builders' manuals of the day.[17] Turning

17. The façade of Palladio's Santo Giorgio is shown on Plate 59 of the second volume of William Kent, *Designs of Inigo Jones* (folio, London, 1727, reprinted 1833). For the pavilion at Stowe, see B. Seeley, *Description of Stowe* (Buckingham, 1777), Plate 2; and *A Dialogue upon the Gardens of the Right Honourable the Lord Viscount Cobham at Stowe in Buckinghamshire* (London, 1748).

to two of Harrison's books, Hoppus' *Palladio* and Ware's *Designs of Inigo Jones and others*, we discover that each contains a design identical with the façade of the Redwood Library, almost line for line, and that the plan of the structure follows closely that given by Ware.[18] (Figures 16-17)

In this his first venture in civil architecture, it must be admitted that Harrison, following the advice of James Gibbs, adhered rather slavishly to the great Palladian books. Although Gibbs actually worked more in baroque tradition than the Palladian, he did strongly recommend the study of classical works to amateurs, and in offering *A Book of Architecture* to the public remarked that "several Persons of Quality . . . were of the opinion that such a Work as this would be of use to such Gentlemen as might be concerned in Building, especially in the remote parts of the Country, where little or no Assistance for Designs can be procured." "For it is not the Bulk of a Fabrick," he insisted, "the Richness and quality of the Materials, the Multiplicity of Lines, nor the Gaudiness of the Finishing, that gives Beauty or Grandeur to a Building, but the Proportion of the Parts to one another and to the Whole, whether entirely plain, or enriched with a few Ornaments properly disposed." [19]

Nearly all of the exterior details of the Library can be found

18. Edward Hoppus, *Palladio* (octavo, 2 vols., London, 1735-36), Headpiece to Book IV; Isaac Ware, *Designs from Inigo Jones and others* (octavo, London, 1740), Plate 43. For a variant design by T. Lightoler, see *The Modern Builder's Assistant* (London, 1757), Plate 61.

19. Gibbs continues: "Such may here be furnished with Draughts of useful and convenient Buildings and proper Ornaments; which may be executed by any Workman who understands Lines, either as here Design'd, or with some Alteration, which may be easily made by a person of Judgment; without which a Variation in Draughts, once well digested, frequently proves a Detriment to the Building, as well as a Disparagement to the Person that gives them. I mention this to caution Gentlemen from suffering any material Change to be made in their Designs by the Forwardness of unskilled Workmen, or the Caprice of ignorant, assuming Pretenders." James Gibbs, *A Book of Architecture*, i-ii.

in three of the volumes Harrison possessed: Hoppus, Ware, and William Kent's *Designs of Inigo Jones*. For example, Lord Burlington had designed a range of three Venetian windows for his villa at Chiswick, the rear façade of which is illustrated in Kent's work. (Figures 19-20) A similar treatment, with more detail, appeared in Ware and as the Headpiece to the Second Book of Hoppus. From these volumes the budding architect took his ideas for the rear façade of the Redwood, which, since the building has been lengthened, has been removed to the side. (Figure 19) Likewise, in designing the front doorway he seems to have borrowed directly from Kent's first volume, not only the panels and lines of the door but the shell and dolphin ornaments for the frieze. Inside, when he came to the bookcases he made them elaborately architectural, possibly relying on a plate in Batty Langley's *Treasury of Designs*.[20]

The resulting building revealed more of the books than of Harrison. Only when the limitations of local materials forced him to do so, did Harrison depart from his English models and use rustication in wood to simulate dressed stone. Yet the effect was striking. The Newporter's cautiousness can be explained upon two grounds: it was his initial attempt at planning; and the structure was admirably adapted to the purpose for which it was intended. It is of the greatest significance that on the threshold of his architectural career Peter Harrison consciously aligned himself with the Earl of Burlington and William Kent in their rebellion against the baroque architecture of Wren and Vanbrugh, under whom,

20. For the rear façade and windows, see William Kent, *Designs of Inigo Jones*, I, Plates 55, 73; and for the bookcases, Batty Langley, *Treasury of Designs* (quarto, London, 1745), Plate 35. Mr. Fiske Kimball, on whose pioneer researches I have leaned heavily, first traced Harrison's sources in "The Colonial Amateurs and Their Models: Peter Harrison," *Architecture*, 53 (1926), 155-60, 185-90, 209. As mentioned in note 10 above, the Harrison inventory of 1775 does not include Langley's *Treasury of Designs*.

ironically and wrongly, he is often said to have served an apprenticeship.[21] By this act he brought to America the Palladian style, which, after a brief interlude, reappeared in a purer Roman form when Thomas Jefferson went back to true classical sources. In the apt phrase of Fiske Kimball: "The Redwood Library was the forerunner of the Virginia Capitol; Harrison the forerunner, as Jefferson was the founder, of American classicism."[22]

Early in 1750 the Redwood Library was completed and stocked with an excellent selection of books purchased in London by John Thomlinson and shipped to Boston in the care of Harrison's friend Stephen Greenleaf. In all, Redwood's gift of £500 bought 206 folio, 128 quarto, 712 octavo, and 251 duodecimo volumes.[23]

The Redwood Library immediately became one of the showplaces of Newport. It was unique on the continent. Visitors were charmed by its beauty and proportions, seldom failing to mention it in their journals. From Cambridge in Massachusetts Lieutenant-Governor Spencer Phips, Colonel Henry and Mrs. Vassall, accompanied by their Quaker acquaintance, James Birket of Antigua, came on a pleasure jaunt in September, 1750, and naturally they visited the new building designed by their friend and fellow-churchman. "They have here a very handsome Library built upon the hill above the Town," noted the West Indian, who particularly admired the prospect of the harbor from its steps.[24] When the

21. After many years of exhaustive research, the late Samuel F. Batchelder could not trace the legend that Harrison was an apprentice under Sir John Vanbrugh at Blenheim any further back than the *Catalogue* of the Redwood Library for 1843. S. F. Batchelder, Peter Harrison: American Colonial Architect, II, which is a typescript of an important unpublished study in the Cambridge Historical Society's collections, now housed in the Widener Library, Harvard University.

22. Kimball, "Colonial Amateurs and Their Models," 209.

23. *A Catalogue of the Books belonging to the Company of the Redwood Library* (Newport, 1764); Mason, *Annals of the Redwood Library*, 36n., 494-514.

24. C. M. Andrews, ed., *Some Cursory Remarks made by James Birket in his Voyage to North America, 1750-51* (New Haven, 1916), 30.

Swiss miniaturist and collector Pierre Eugène du Simitière visited Newport in 1767 he was so greatly impressed with the Redwood that he made a charming watercolor painting of it in his sketchbook. (Figure 7)

More important, because of its contemporary circulation, was the detailed description of the Library given by Dr. William Douglass of Boston in his widely-read *Summary of the British Settlements in North America*. It is the more interesting because this dour Scot could seldom find anything in the colonies that pleased him, but perhaps the explanation lies in the fact that when he visited Newport in 1750 his countryman Dr. Thomas Moffatt, an intimate of Peter Harrison, was librarian of the Redwood and showed him around the building. After praising the generosity of Abraham Redwood, Douglass applauds the structure, describing its architectural details in terms he knew would arouse interest and understanding in the "Better Sort" who bought his book. "I shall give you some Account of it," he remarks, in the hope "that this may be of Exemplary Use to our other Provinces and Colonies:

The Building for the Library consists of one large Room, where the Books are kept, 36 Foot long, 26 Foot Broad, and 19 Foot high, with two small Offices adjoining. The Principal or West Front is a Pediment and Portico of 4 Columns after the Doric Order; the whole Entablature of which, runs quite around the Building. The two Offices are placed as Wings, one on each Side of the Portico, and connected with the Body of the Building, so as to form two half-Pediments proceeding from the lower Part of the Entablature. These two Wings, besides the Conveniences they afford, have a very good Effect in extending as well as adding Variety to this Front. The East Front consists of a plain Dorick Pediment supported by a Rustick Arcade of three Arches, in the Recesses of which are plac'd three Venetian Windows after the Ionic Order. The Outside of the whole Building is of Rustick Work,[25] and stands on a Base about

25. The specifications called for a sheathing of "Pine Plank worked in imitation of Rustick" or stone-work. See Appendix E, and Figures 7, 15.

5 Feet high from the Ground, and the Entrance is by a Flight of Steps the whole Width of the Portico.[26]

So closely does this description fit the terms of the contract that one has the ineradicable impression that the architect must have accompanied the physician when he toured the building and explained its leading features to him. When the *Summary* appeared in 1752 Harrison bought and treasured a copy, as well he might, since its description of the Library is probably the most detailed in print of any pre-revolutionary building in America.

The Directors of the Library rewarded John Thomlinson and Stephen Greenleaf in 1750 for their efforts in procuring the books by making them honorary members. Conspicuously they failed to do anything for Peter Harrison. He had undertaken the preparation of the plans as a public service owed by a gentleman to his community; he had no thought of compensation. It is curious, nevertheless, that nowhere in the Company's minutes is there a scrap of evidence that he was ever officially thanked for his great and generous work. One thing is clear—Peter Harrison never became a member of the Library; the Company's fine callousness provides a sufficient explanation. The building itself was ample reward. Moreover, he had no need to use its books, because he was developing in his own library one of the best collections in the English colonies.[27]

The year 1748-49 proved to be one of the most crowded and active of Harrison's whole career. As we have seen, his first real

26. William Douglass, *A Summary, Historical and Political, of the . . . British Settlements in North America* (Boston, 1747-52), II, 101. The section on Newport was written about 1750.

27. The Redwood *Catalogue* of 1764 does not list any architectural works that he might have used in drawing up his plans. Moreover, the books arrived after construction was finished. Compare Harrison's inventory (Appendix C), with Mason, *Annals of the Redwood Library*, 37, 38, 41, 42, 44-47, 49.

beginning at domestic life and the urgency of his business affairs were enough to absorb any average man's time and energy. Superintending the erection of the Redwood Library, although time-consuming, he regarded as a "delightful recreation." Diverting also was the preparation of the plan of a summerhouse for the Redwood estate which he took from a design in James Gibbs's *A Book of Architecture*.[28] (Figures 21-22) Had he so desired, numerous commissions to design private dwellings would have easily come his way, but, with one or two possible exceptions in the case of friends, Peter Harrison remained exclusively the gentleman architect.[29]

The word went out among colonial Anglicans that a member of Trinity Church, Newport, was "a Gent. of good Judgment in Architecture," and before long Peter Harrison received from the Reverend Henry Caner of King's Chapel, Boston, a letter dated April 5, 1749. "As they design with all convenient Expedition to proceed," the committee for building a new church had asked him, the rector artlessly wrote, "to acquaint you that they would esteem it a Favour if you would oblige them with a Draught of a handsome Church agreeable to the Limitts hereinafter assigned." After enumerating the limits, he added a paragraph that does as

---

28. The summerhouse is now on the grounds of the Redwood Library. Gibbs, *A Book of Architecture*, Plate 80, and Figures 21-22 of the present work.

29. Three Newport houses of this period have been attributed to Peter Harrison: the Bull House (now destroyed), the Banister House (much altered) at One Mile Corner, and the famous Bowler-Vernon House. These dwellings were all sheathed with rusticated woodwork, somewhat like that of the Redwood Library, and are the only structures in Newport so treated. As a connection by marriage of John Banister and an intimate of Charles and Metcalf Bowler, Harrison may have agreed to do them a friendly service. The late Norman M. Isham, the most careful student of Rhode Island architecture, used to tell his classes that he believed Harrison to have been the architect for these three houses, because the quality of their designs and workmanship surpassed anything the carpenter-architects of Newport ever produced. There is no documentary evidence to aid in clarifying this problem. Conversation with Antoinette Downing, June 28, 1947.

much credit to the taste and judgment of the committee as to the bold casualness with which they laid out several months' work for Mr. Harrison:

As the cheif Beauty and Strength of Building depends upon a due Proportion of the several Members to each other, the Gentlemen of the Committee are encouraged to make this Application to you, whom they have often heard mentioned with Advantage for a particular Judgment and Taste in Things of this Kind, and for the Knowledge you have acquired by travelling and Observation. We do not require any great Expense of Ornament, but chiefly aim at Symmetry and Proportion, which we entirely submit to your Judgment.[30]

The committee really wanted a rough-stone edifice with one tier of windows on a side, but the members hesitated not to request "a prospect of each Sort, one with a single tier of windows and the other with two"—that is, a church with and without a balcony. To Peter Harrison were left such matters as the size, height, and ornament of the steeple, the committee requiring only that he submit "a Draught, . . . together with a Ground Platt." Should he be able to accommodate them, concluded Mr. Caner, the gentlemen of the committee would deem it "a very great Favour"—as indeed it was.

Peter Harrison was no stranger among Boston Anglicans. He was acquainted with at least two of the committee, Charles Apthorp and Dr. Silvester Gardiner, while its clerk, Barlow Trecothick, was a personal friend and business connection. Trecothick's London partner, John Thomlinson, who had contributed heavily to the undertaking, was managing the drive for funds in

30. The similarity between Mr. Caner's first sentence and the following translation from Palladio is striking: "As for the beauty of an edifice, it consists of an exact proportion of the parts within themselves, and of each part with the whole." The gentlemen of the committee were themselves familiar enough with works of architecture to recognize in Harrison a good architect. Rev. Mr. Caner to Captain Harrison, Apr. 5, 1749, King's Chapel Parish House, Boston; Giacomo Leoni, *Palladio* (London, 1721), 1.

England. It is more than likely these two gentlemen recommended Harrison to the building committee.[31]

Here was a truly formidable commission. Any master-builder could lay out a plain frame Congregational meetinghouse, but no "architect" in New England except Harrison possessed the learning and the talent necessary for planning an elaborate Episcopal church of the kind specified by the building committee for King's Chapel. He was being asked to design the first large cut-stone structure in the colonies and to fit his plans to a lot that he had no opportunity to examine. The honor was great, and he could hardly refuse the many friends who sponsored him. So he took up the challenge.

This acceptance the committee members had anticipated, expecting immediate results as well, for in May they began to buy building materials, "being every Day encouraged to expect their Plan," and in July commenced work on the foundations.

When Harrison first sat down at his drawingboard to lay out King's Chapel he had before him only the few "Limitts" mentioned in the rector's letter:

The Length of the Church from West to East, including the Steeple, is to be 120 feet, besides which there will be 10 feet allowed for a Chancel. The breadth is to be 65 feet 8 inches. The Ground has a Declivity of about 5 feet from West to East.... The Building is to be of rough Stone.[32]

31. Other wealthy and influential pewholders of King's Chapel with whom Peter Harrison was well acquainted were: Sir Henry Frankland, John Erving, John Powell, Charles Paxton, John Reed, Robert Auchmuty, Henry Vassall, and Stephen Greenleaf. Henry Wilder Foote, *Annals of King's Chapel* (Boston, 1881-96), II, 62, 69-70, 585-601, 607-9. At this time John Thomlinson was petitioning Parliament for the privilege of purchasing Bank Annuities "at 4£ per cent, to the amount of 11,328£," for John Erving and Charles Apthorp. Leo F. Stock, ed., *Proceedings and Debates of the British Parliament respecting North America* (Washington, 1924—), V, 456.

32. Caner to P. Harrison, Apr. 5, 1749, King's Chapel.

So long as he avoided needless expense, he was free to plan any kind of an edifice that suited his taste.

With a confidence born of his success with the Redwood Library, Peter Harrison now boldly decided on a set of designs that would express his own individuality, yet at the same time adhere to academic canons. He might adapt a suggestion or two from the books, perhaps borrow a detail or two, but the finished composition would be his own. Bearing in mind the committee's injunction that symmetry and proportion rather than expensive ornament ought to govern his work, he provided an exceedingly plain exterior for the body of the church, which, in addition to the decision to use rough local rather than finished Portland stone, imparted an American quality to the structure at the outset. (Figure 23) To insure proper lighting for the galleries he gave the north and south flanks of the church two tiers of windows, suggested no doubt by Plate 24 in *A Book of Architecture* (Figure 24), while on the east end he placed one of those Palladian windows that were so much in vogue in England. (Figure 25)

Most of the details of the interior orders come from the *Rules for Drawing* by James Gibbs. On one plan can be found models for the Ionic and Corinthian colonnades, while the balustrade for the altar-rail appears in the upper right-hand corner of another.[33] From two plates in Batty Langley's *Treasury of Designs* Harrison apparently drew his inspiration for the altar-piece, but the solution was that of the designer, not the copyist. The successful combining of all these elements and the strict attention paid to the measure-

33. By orthodox Palladians James Gibbs was considered one of the bad boys of architecture, because of his leanings toward the baroque. His *Rules for Drawing the Several Parts of Architecture* (small folio, London, 1732; 2d edn., 1738), however, provided the clearest, simplest, and most useful instructions for working out the several orders according to classical rules. Peter Harrison consulted his Gibbs freely in such matters, as in the case mentioned above. See *Rules for Drawing*, Plates 2, 62, and Figure 25.

ments and proportions of the orders produced one of the most elegantly-designed church interiors in colonial America.[34] (Figure 25)

"The Steeple and Spire, for Bigness, Height, and Ornament is left with you to determine," wrote Caner, and, because he had been restricted in his plans for the body of the church, Harrison "pulled out all the stops" when he came to the steeple. He conceived a tower of unusual depth, enclosed by a porch of twelve Ionic columns, which, being twenty-five feet high, brought the roof of the porch even with that of the body of the church. Such a treatment could be found nowhere else in America. He carried the entablature of the porch along the front of the building, where it was supported on each side by pilasters of the same order. (Figure 1) He thus strove to produce a façade architecture by emphasizing the front at the expense of the sides and rear. The tower was so rich that Harrison had to create the illusion of fastening it to a building equally elaborate, an impression further enhanced by the extension of the four-feet, two-inches balustrade all the way around the building.[35]

The plans for the spire were particularly ambitious. Since the tower was to be twenty-six feet square "from out to out," and its walls four feet thick at the base, it is evident that a masonry spire of considerable height and weight was contemplated.[36] "Accord-

34. See two designs for Tuscan altar-pieces in Batty Langley, *Treasury of Designs* (1740, 1741 eds.), Plates 108 and 109. He took the cherubs from another source not located. When the interior of King's Chapel is compared with the somewhat similar interior of Richard Munday's Trinity Church (1728) at Newport, the superiority of the former is obvious. Norman M. Isham, *Trinity Church in Newport, Rhode Island* (Boston, 1936) contains several excellent views.

35. Harrison's original plan was followed when the present portico of King's Chapel, with its wooden columns, was built around the tower, 1785-87. At the same time a wooden balustrade was placed around the roof. Sketch of King's Chapel in 1833 at the end of Foote, *King's Chapel*, II. No trace of Harrison's plans can be found in the church records.

36. Foote, *King's Chapel*, II, 96.

ing to the original design of the architect," which was in existence as late as 1784, he intended to erect upon the block type cornice which crowned the tower "an elegant and lofty steeple of two square stories and an octagonal spire. The first story is to be of the Ionick order, with 16 fluted coupled columns and pilasters, 19 inches in diameter. The second story, of the Corinthian order, formed of 8 fluted single columns, 14 inches in diameter. The spire rising above, to be finished in the richest manner. The columns with their entablature, which projects from the body of the steeple, to support highly finished and ornamental urns." [37] Four windows with carved stone frames were planned for the steeple, as well as thirty-two stone urns or vases to go on the balustrade.[38] King's Chapel tower and spire as their designer conceived them were to be as elaborate and imposing as those of any church then existing in London itself! [39]

Throughout the spring and summer of 1749 Harrison worked steadily on the drawings for King's Chapel. For a diversion the former sea captain assisted his brother and other members of the colony's committee in the erection of Beavertail Lighthouse on Conanicut Island at the entrance to Newport harbor. It would have been just like him to offer to draw up plans for this sorely-

37. Quoted by Noah Webster from the *Geographical Gazetteer of 1784*, in *American Magazine*, New York (October, 1788), 763.

38. Although the plans have disappeared, some idea of the elegance of this conception may be had from the estimates for the "Free Stone Work" submitted by the famous Ralph Allen of Bath in accordance with Peter Harrison's specifications. At the suggestion of Thomas Gunter, on November 22, 1750, a letter was sent to Allen at Prior Park soliciting his support of the King's Chapel undertaking. He responded more than generously by offering to present all the "Bath Stone" needed for the building and to procure trained stoneworkers to cross to Boston and turn the stone. The value of his gift was set at £1,000. Foote, *King's Chapel*, II, 90-91, 95-97 (for the estimate). Austin Dobson's delightful essay on Allen in his *Eighteenth Century Vignettes* is well known.

39. For example, compare King's Chapel with St. Martin's-in-the-Fields, the two plans for a Circular Church, St. Mary Le Strand, and Marylebone Chapel in Gibbs, *A Book of Architecture*, Plates 1, 7, 9, 10, 14, 15, 21, 29-31.

needed aid to navigation.[40] He and his wife appeared at the August term of the Superior Court to lodge a complaint against Nicholas Otis, "Taylor, alias Mariner," for failing to prosecute his appeal from the decision of the Inferior Court of Common Pleas made against him in May in an action of trespass and ejectment concerning one of Harrison's houses at the east end of Pelham's Wharf. It was a hectic month fittingly climaxed by excitement and worry over the birth of a son, named Thomas after his grandfather, on August 22, 1749.[41]

Soon the gentlemen of King's Chapel "began to be very solicitous for the Plan." Finally, in reply to some prodding from the Reverend Mr. Caner, the architect wrote a brief answer (Figure 8), one which is doubly valuable because it affords a glimpse of his architectural credo:

Newport, September 15th, 1749

Sir,—Since I first undertook to draw a Design for the New Church, many things has unexpectedly occurr'd to prevent me from finishing it in the time you requested. However have at last compleated it; and now send you per the Post Rider all the Plans and Elevations (as mentioned below) which I should be glad to hear answer your expectations, and that no material Alteration is made in the Execution, as it is very possible by that means the Symmetry of the Whole may be destroy'd.

The Body of the Building (as you directed) is as Plain as the Order of it will possibly admitt of; but the Steeple is fully Decorated, and I believe will have a beautifull effect. The Inside is likewise design'd Plain, and as regular as can be contriv'd from the Dimensions you limited me to. From these hints, you may perhaps be able to answer the Objections of such the Committee and others, who may not be conversant with Drawings, or have not a Taste in Things of this Nature. I am, Sir,

Your most humble Servt.

PETER HARRISON

40. Colonial Records of Rhode Island, VI, 47, R. I. Archives; *American Magazine* (October, 1788), 763.

41. Superior Court Records, August Term, 1749, Newport County Court House; Arnold, *Vital Records of Rhode Island*, X, 504.

The Plan—
The Elevation of the West Front
The Elevation of the East Front
The Section—Breadthways
The Plans of the Steeple
The Plans of the Pews [42]

Peter Harrison was an unusually mild-mannered man, and this polite letter hardly reflects his asperity at being lectured to and then rushed on the job—a gratis job at that. More apparent are a conscious pride in his achievement and an evident concern lest the pure classical turn given to his designs, especially those for the steeple, suffer in the hands of a lay committee, which might not "have a Taste in Things of this Nature," or recognize that these plans with their elaborate ornament represented a distinct innovation in American ecclesiastical architecture. Possibly he also spoke from experience with the Redwood Library. Fortunately, Mr. Caner was able to assure him that the committee was "well-pleased" with his efforts, would follow them as faithfully as possible, and that when it was within its power the members desired to make some further acknowledgment of his "Favour." [43] This power seems never to have been vouchsafed to the committee, and the Newport gentleman may have reflected that as the Redwood Library was his contribution to literary culture, so the plans for King's Chapel were a tribute exclusively to the greater glory of God.

The six carefully prepared drawings he submitted were most unusual for their day and indicate that Peter Harrison was far more than an amateur in the methods with which he approached

---

42. From the manuscript in the Parish House of King's Chapel through the courtesy of the Reverend Palfrey Perkins. Foote prints this letter with some variations, *King's Chapel*, II, 77-79, 82.

43. *Ibid.*, 83.

his architectural work.[44] In dealing with measurements and proportions he was always rigidly precise. Where an amateur would have been content to make the balustrade for the steeple portico four feet high, Harrison correctly made it four feet, two inches. His drawings did please the committee, so much, in fact, that they ordered the plan and an elevation engraved so that copies could be used in soliciting subscriptions both in America and in England. Harrison might be pardoned for the justifiable pride he took in having his plans engraved as well as for his great satisfaction in the news that Ralph Allen (after whom Fielding drew his Squire Allworthy) had written to Thomas Gunter of the Vestry, saying "I . . . have seen the Draught of the New Church, which . . . I much approve," and had implemented his praise with an offer to furnish "all the [Bristol] freestone that will be wanting for the Ornaments of your Building." [45]

Work on the church began early in 1750, when stone was brought by water from the North Common of Braintree, where it had been prepared by heating with fire and broken by dropping cannon balls on it. This is the first recorded use of Quincy granite. The masons, Messrs. Ray, Derham, and Ball, by their slowness at work, proved a sore trial to the committee. Moreover, so great was the expense incurred in erecting the structure that Peter Harrison's fine steeple was not undertaken, nor were any of the exterior decorations placed on the edifice. In 1787 the portico and balustrade were executed according to the plan—but entirely of wood,

44. John Hawks produced only three drawings for Tryon's Palace at New Bern, N. C., 1767-1770: a ground-floor plan; the upper-floor plan; and the main elevation. Alonzo T. Dill, Jr., "Tryon's Palace," *North Carolina Historical Review*, 19 (1942), 119-67, and plates. Colonial architectural drawings were usually very crude, like those for the Chaloner and Ayrault houses at Newport. Master builders like Benjamin Wyatt and Richard Munday ordinarily made only one draught or plan. Fiske Kimball, *Domestic Architecture of the American Colonies and of the Early Republic* (New York, 1927), Figures 32, 45.

45. Foote, *King's Chapel*, II, 95.

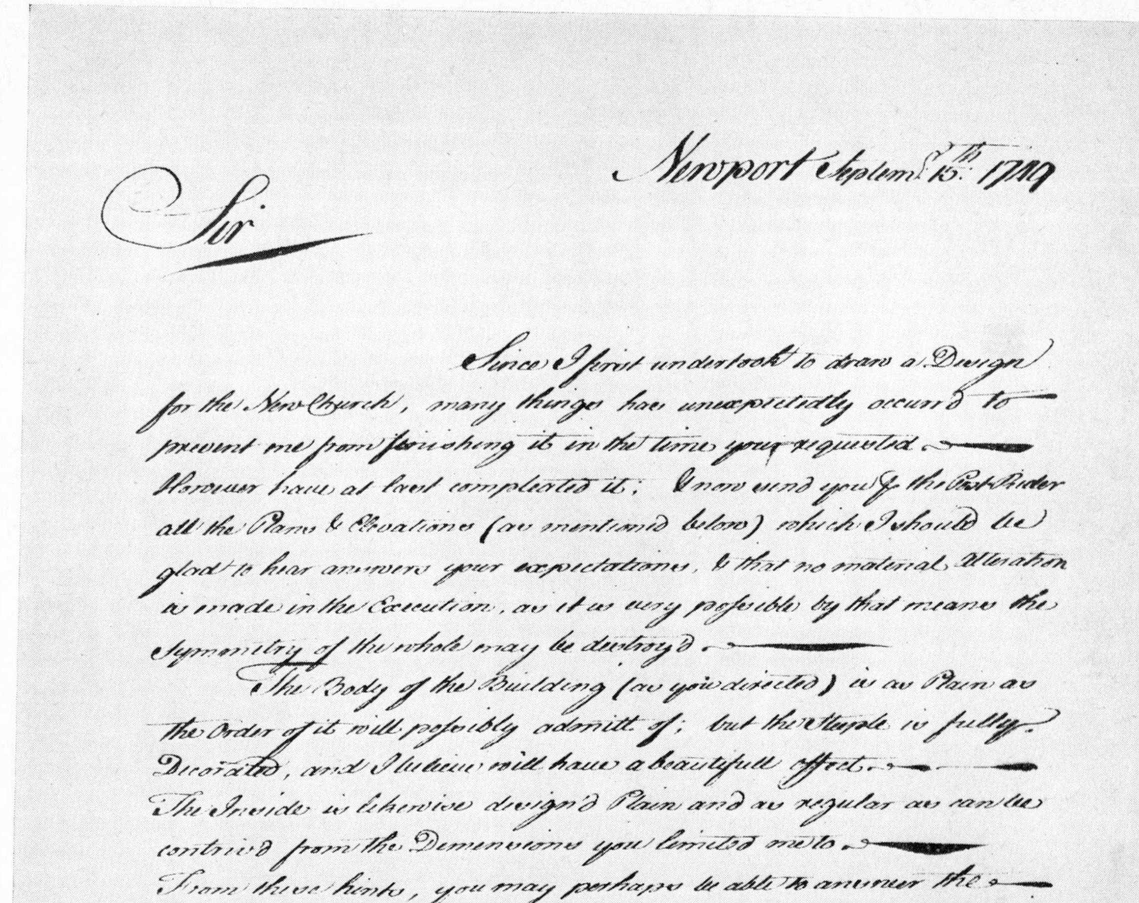

FIGURE 8. Peter Harrison's letter to the Reverend Henry Caner transmitting the plans for King's Chapel, September 15, 1749. *Courtesy of the Reverend Palfrey Perkins*

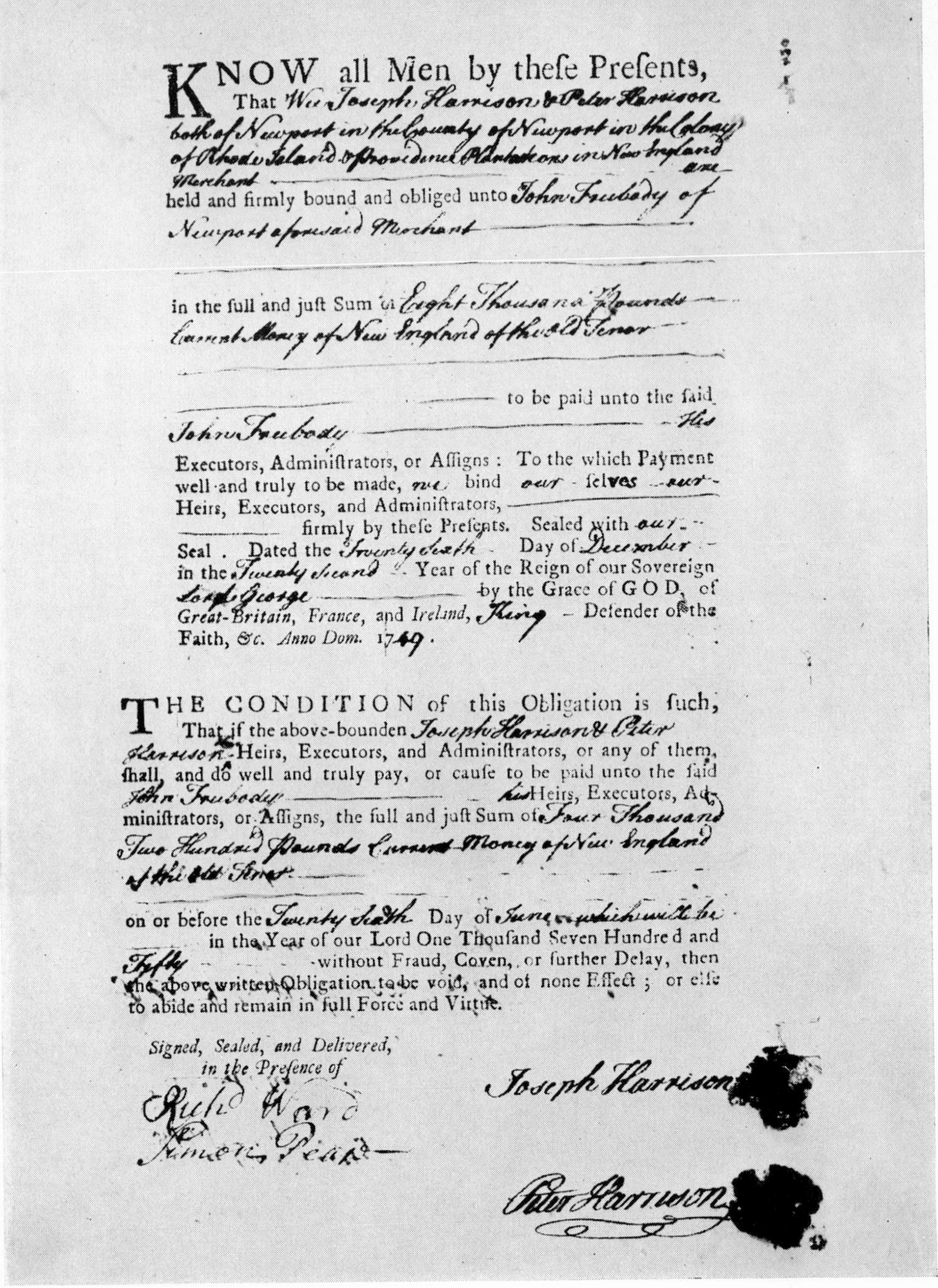

KNOW all Men by these Presents, That We Joseph Harrison & Peter Harrison both of Newport in the County of Newport in the Colony of Rhode Island & Providence Plantations in New England Merchant are held and firmly bound and obliged unto John Freebody of Newport aforesaid Merchant

in the full and just Sum of Eight Thousand Pounds Current Money of New England of the old Tenor

to be paid unto the said John Freebody His Executors, Administrators, or Assigns: To the which Payment well and truly to be made, we bind our selves our Heirs, Executors, and Administrators, firmly by these Presents. Sealed with our Seal. Dated the Twenty sixth Day of December in the Twenty second Year of the Reign of our Sovereign Lord George by the Grace of GOD, of Great-Britain, France, and Ireland, King Defender of the Faith, &c. Anno Dom. 1749.

THE CONDITION of this Obligation is such, That if the above-bounden Joseph Harrison & Peter Harrison Heirs, Executors, and Administrators, or any of them, shall, and do well and truly pay, or cause to be paid unto the said John Freebody his Heirs, Executors, Administrators, or Assigns, the full and just Sum of Four Thousand Two Hundred Pounds Current Money of New England of the old Tenor

on or before the Twenty sixth Day of June which will be in the Year of our Lord One Thousand Seven Hundred and Fifty without Fraud, Coven, or further Delay, then the above written Obligation to be void, and of none Effect; or else to abide and remain in full Force and Virtue.

Signed, Sealed, and Delivered, in the Presence of

Richd Ward

Simon Pease

Joseph Harrison

Peter Harrison

FIGURE 9. A debt that ran for over twenty years: the note of Joseph and Peter Harrison to John Freebody for a loan of £8000, December 22, 1749. *Courtesy of the Newport Historical Society* since true to its original premise, the committee did not feel the need for "any great Expense of Ornament." It is doubtful if Harrison ever saw King's Chapel while it was being built. Almost five years passed from the date the plans were received until the church was sufficiently near completion to be opened for services on August 21, 1754. Although over £7405 sterling had been expended by 1758, King's Chapel was then far from finished; in fact, to the great loss of American architecture it was never finished.[46]

Reports of Peter Harrison's success with the Redwood Library and of the magnificence of the rising structure of King's Chapel circulated beyond New England to a colonial metropolis that did not have the good fortune of numbering an accomplished architect among its citizens. On June 14, 1751, the South Carolina Assembly passed an act dividing Charles Town into two parishes, and appointing nine gentlemen as "Commissioners or supervisors" to build a church "with a steeple" and "a ring of bells" in the newly-created parish of St. Michael.[47] No direct evidence concerning the architect of this famous church has ever been found, and only recently clear proof that its builder, Samuel Cardy, definitely did not design it has come to light.[48]

46. "Report on the Building Stones of the United States," *U.S. Tenth Census*, X (1884), 283-84; George P. Merrill, *Stones for Building and Decoration* (New York, 1891), 2; Foote, *King's Chapel*, II, 88, 93, 95, 115, 116-67, 404.

47. The commissioners were: Charles Pinckney, Alexander van Bussen, Edward Fenwicke, William Bull, Jr., Andrew Rutledge, Isaac Mazyck, Benjamin Smith, Jordan Roche, and James Irving. T. Cooper and D. J. McChord, eds., *Statutes at Large of South Carolina* (Charleston, 1838-41), VII, 80.

48. Beatrice St. Julien Ravenel writes in her excellent *Architects of Charleston* (Charleston, 1945, pp. 27-29) that "No matter whose the plans, they were not followed slavishly," and she concludes that Samuel Cardy was only the builder, not the designer. Recently discovered documents, including Cardy's receipt books and data on building materials, seem to indicate that Cardy was the builder but definitely not the architect of St. Michael's Church. These papers were not made available to me, although it is expected that they will soon be published. *South Carolina Historical and Genealogical Magazine*, 46 (1945), 180.

From his first years in the New World Peter Harrison had connections with Charles Town. He was well-known in the city, having visited there on business in 1742 and as recently as 1747. The House of Harrison, moreover, made a specialty of the Carolina trade. Peter's social relations with Gabriel Manigault, one of the two or three most influential men in the province, would naturally have made it possible for him to meet other leading citizens, including Isaac Mazyck, one of the building commissioners and, like Manigault, of Huguenot background.[49]

Himself one of the leading gentry of Newport, Peter Harrison would have been sought out immediately by the constantly increasing number of prominent South Carolinians arriving at Newport each summer for the benefit of their health. Nor could they have failed after viewing the Redwood Library to carry home accounts of its unique classic charm and of the abilities of its designer to those whose knowledge was confined to the description in the second volume of Dr. William Douglass' *Summary*. Intercourse, both commercial and social, became increasingly frequent between the two colonial cities after the Peace of Aix-la-Chapelle in 1748.[50] It is also probable that one or more of the engravings of Harrison's plans for King's Chapel, which were going the rounds, reached Charles Town and there aroused as much admira-

49. Peter to Elizabeth Harrison, Charles Town, Mar. 23, 1747, Van Buren Papers.

50. The most striking evidence of the intimate connection between Charles Town and Newport is the number of gravestones erected for South Carolinians in Trinity Church yard. Three of the "supervisors," Andrew Rutledge, Benjamin Smith, and William Bull, Jr., visited Newport after 1758. They may also have come before this date, when the local newspaper first recorded summer arrivals. *Newport Mercury*, Aug. 3, 1767; June 18, 1770; June 6, 1774. See, in general, Carl Bridenbaugh, "Colonial Newport as a Summer Resort," Rhode Island Historical Society, *Collections*, 26 (1933), 1-23; and "Charlestonians at Newport, 1767-1775," *S. C. Hist. & Gen. Magazine*, 41 (1940), 43-47; *Providence Gazette*, July 28, 1770.

tion as it did in Ralph Allen and his more sophisticated circle in England.

Harrison's interest in the building of Charles Town was of long standing. His first visit to the city occurred during the slow process of rebuilding after the great fire of 1740, which destroyed "the most valuable Part of the Town." Absorbed as he was in architecture, he could hardly have failed to take an interest in the radical new building code, especially the provisions requiring all new buildings to be constructed of brick or stone and requiring the demolition of every frame structure.[51] On his return in 1747 he must have noticed that, despite the improvements of the last five years, many frame buildings were still standing. And the feature of the city's physical appearance which most excited his attention would naturally have been the rebuilding of the city's walls and the six small bastions or fortifications, for Charles Town was British America's only walled and fortified city.[52]

Like the gentlemen of King's Chapel, those of Charles Town had undoubtedly heard Peter Harrison mentioned as a man noted "for a particular Judgment and Taste" in architecture as well as for a vast knowledge acquired by travel and observation. After all, who else in "this remote part" of the Empire, "where little or no Assistance for Designs can be procured," would be better able to produce a set of plans for a handsome Anglican church?[53] It not only seems logical but highly probable that in the summer of

51. Bridenbaugh, *Cities in the Wilderness*, 371-72.

52. Under Charles Town news the *Pennsylvania Gazette* of June 23, 1743, reported that "Two new Forts are just finish'd in this Town, two others pretty forward, and two more are building on the other Side of the Harbour." See Plates 10, 11, in Bridenbaugh, *Cities in the Wilderness*, 310, and especially the view of Charles Town from the water in the copy of the *Atlantic Neptune* (London, n. d.) at the Mariner's Museum, Newport News, Va.

53. A possible exception was Dr. John Kearsley who designed Christ Church at Philadelphia. He never undertook another building after 1731, and, moreover, the master-builder, James Porteus, is now thought to have had a large share in making the Christ Church plans. Bridenbaugh, *Cities in the Wilderness*, 306.

1751 some fellow-Anglican from Charles Town bespoke the New-porter's services in designing a church for the new parish of St. Michael. The flat terrain would present no problem, as Harrison recalled it; so he pored over his books for an inspiration and for details suitable for use in his design. The two works of James Gibbs, *A Book of Architecture* and *Rules for Drawing*, seem to have aided him most, as in the case of King's Chapel. Yet his plan for St. Michael's is only Gibbsian in general appearance; it conforms to no single pattern that can be traced to the books even though the main source seems to be Plate 14 of *A Book of Architecture*. (Figure 26)

He must have made rapid progress with the plans, because the *South-Carolina Gazette* for October 23, 1751, announced that Isaac Mazyck and Benjamin Smith, "in whose hands the plan is lodg'd," were "ready to agree" with workmen. Negotiations having been completed, on February 22, 1752, the newspaper carried the following announcement:

The Commissioners for building the Church of St. Michael in this Town, having waited upon his Excellency the Governor to desire that He would be pleased to lay the first stone; on Monday last, His Excellency, attended by several members of His Majesty's Hon. Council, and other Gentlemen, was pleased to proceed to the Spot, and lay the same accordingly and thereon a Sum of Money; a Stone was then laid by each of the Gentlemen that attended His Excellency, followed by the loud acclamations of a numerous Concourse of People that assembled to see the Ceremony; after which the Company proceeded to Mr. Gordon's [Tavern], where a handsome Entertainment was provided by the Commissioners: Dinner over, His Majesty's Health was drank, followed by a discharge of the Cannon at Granville's Bastion, then the Healths of all the Royal Family, and other loyal Toasts; and this Day was concluded with peculiar Pleasure and Satisfaction. This Church will be built on the Plan of one of Mr. Gibson's Designs; and 'tis tho't, will exhibit a fine Piece of Architecture when compleated: The Steeple being designed much larger than that of St. Philip's, will have a fine Set of Bells.

The Church Supervisors of Charles Town honored their community, if the supposition is correct, when they chose the first architect of the colonies to design St. Michael's. There was no need for Harrison to supervise construction of the edifice when he sent down such a complete set of plans. Samuel Cardy performed this work admirably, and when, after some changes in the plan of the portico, the interruption of a hurricane, and numerous other delays, St. Michael's was opened for worship in 1761, it was indeed one of the noblest churches of America.[54] In drawing the plans Peter Harrison characteristically adapted the building to its locality; he designed a small community church, like many of those of Gibbs, rather than a great city church. King's Chapel would have been out of place in a small city like Charles Town. In considering both of these edifices, however, one is constantly struck by the accuracy of the detail and the attention paid to the proportions of the orders. It is also significant that these are the only two churches of the pre-revolutionary period, 1730-1776, which had a colossal portico included in the design. Peter Harrison is the only colonial architect who is known to have used this Gibbsian feature in his plans for civic and ecclesiastical buildings. This service performed as a gesture for his fellow-churchmen could easily have passed without contemporary mention, as was so often the case in the colonies.

Completion of the plans for St. Michael's brought to a close Peter Harrison's first ventures in architecture, and for nearly a decade his business, domestic affairs, and finally the coming of the French and Indian War drew his attention to other matters.

54. St. Michael's and King's Chapel were among the few churches in the colonies at this time to have a portico of the classic type.

III

Broad Acres and Distinction

AT NEWPORT in the mid-eighteenth century, as in the mother country, new wealth inevitably seated itself upon old acres. Attachment to the soil and to the distinction that accrued to its possessor had always been the first love of Rhode Islanders, but economic necessity had driven them down to the sea. At the first opportunity, however, merchant grandees hastened to acquire country estates upon which they might lavish their wealth and to which they might resort when they tired of town and counting house.

Peter Harrison's marriage to Elizabeth Pelham brought him the control of a large piece of land in the center of Newport with seven houses standing on it and a fine estate, called Leamington Farm, facing the harbor about half a mile from the town. Pride and an understandable resentment of the opposition to his marriage seem to have made the captain decide to "beach" himself after one last voyage to lay the foundations of future life as a merchant. When he stepped ashore in 1748, he was determined to give up his nautical life, to establish his family in the "handsome and genteel manner" he so admired, and to imitate the ideal of the English country gentry by settling down to agriculture, ease, and Madeira.

Upon his arrival in Newport and during the time that John Stevens, the stonecutter, and other workmen were preparing the

Mansion House, the Harrisons, as previously stated, probably lived in town with Madam Pelham.[1] It is not known just when they moved to the farm on Brenton's Cove, but it must have been in 1749. During the early fifties Peter found himself free from concerns of a public nature for the first time since his marriage, and these years he energetically devoted to his business and home life. The divorce was complete by December, 1751, for he did not even join with his old Newport mates in forming the Fellowship Club, a benevolent society to provide for the needy families of commanders of vessels.[2]

The Harrison Farm, as Elizabeth's entailed property on Brenton's Cove was eventually known, soon engrossed as much of her husband's attention as his mercantile partnership with Joseph. In what condition he found the land is not recorded, but he devoted himself assiduously to improving it and in so doing displayed a remarkable knowledge of agriculture and the capacity to put it into practice. He applied, with measurable success, lore learned at Hornsea and Wyeston and methods gleaned from his manuals, for among the books he had selected from London stalls were a volume on "Improving clayey grounds," "Hale's Husbandry," "Barrow's Industry," and "The Gentleman's Farriery."[3] He was one of the first in New England, if not the colonies, to follow the injunctions of Jethro Tull and Lord Townsend by planting turnips, cultivating potatoes, carrots, and other vegetables, and by growing grasses.[4]

1. John Stevens, famous for his carved gravestones, submitted a bill to Peter Harrison on October 11, 1747, for "poynting your chimny and Stuff, to Whiting your house, to mending plastering and stuff, to laying out one hearth, to morter for do, to poynting one chimny," totalling £11.15.0, which was promptly paid in cash on Peter's return from England. Account Book, 282, in possession of John Howard Benson of the Rhode Island School of Design.

2. Joseph Harrison did not join the Fellowship Club either. *Newport Historical Magazine*, 4 (1883-84), 163-67.

3. See inventory of books, Appendix B.

4. Harrison improved on the husbandry of his native Yorkshire, for in 1770 Arthur Young described the East Riding "as good turnip land, but their culture

In husbandry, as in architecture and military engineering, he was an innovator in America.

Under Peter's loving care and management, his wife's estate became a showplace noted for fine prospects across the harbor towards his fortifications on Goat Island. As time passed he saw to the enclosing of the one hundred and sixty acres, chiefly with those neatly and patiently constructed "substantial Stone Fences" found only on Rhode Island; although at great labor and expense, the bounding of certain fields was done with wooden fences requiring over 3,000 cedar rails and posts.[5] Around the "spacious Mansion House," for which he had brought over a complete set of English furnishings on his last voyage, all necessary and convenient outbuildings were erected, including a large barn and a coach house. Adjacent to the great house was a beautiful garden, while on another side was planted an orchard numbering well over a hundred apple and other fruit trees. At some distance across the fields lay a woodland tract which furnished firewood for the mansion's many fireplaces.[6]

So successful was Peter Harrison's husbandry that he earned a reputation throughout New England for "his knowledge in agriculture." [7] He calculated the annual sterling income from the farm as follows:

---

is so wretchedly defective . . . that they had better have let it alone." Quoted by William Cunningham, *The Growth of English Industry and Commerce in Modern Times* (Cambridge, 1892), 367.

5. During the British occupation of Newport, Hessian troops quartered at the Harrison Farm tore up for fuel this number of rails and posts, valued at £75 sterling. Over £100 worth of stone from the walls was used for ships' ballast or in building redoubts. Hermione Cargey's Schedule of Losses, A. O. 12: ff. 395-96; A. O. 13: Bundle 68.

6. Firewood for dwellers in Newport was always imported and very expensive; only a rich gentleman enjoyed the convenience of a woodlot. The Hessians cut down seventy of the fruit trees, which were valued at £1.0.0 each. A. O. 12: f. 396; A. O. 13: Bundle 68.

7. The Particulars lost at Newhaven, etc., and letter of J. Harrison to Sir

25 Tons of Hay	£ 56. 5. 0
300 Bushels of Potatoes at 4/6	67.10. 0
200 Bushels of Turnips at 2/3	22.10. 0
Cabbages and other Vegetables	26. 0. 0
	£172. 5. 0

In addition he kept a herd of cows, raised ten to fifteen hogs a year, and maintained from three to four hundred poultry.[8] When he moved to New Haven in 1766, Harrison rented this lucrative estate "well stockt, and under the best Cultivation, by three year leases, at 300 [Spanish] dollars by the Year, and the Tenant besides made annually £10 worth of Stone Wall." He valued the farm lands, buildings, and stock in 1774 at £4,000 sterling. With £172.5.0 sterling from the farm, £140.13.4 currency in rents from seven dwellings in town, and profits from his commercial ventures, the merchant lived in affluence, maintaining his family in the style its social position demanded.[9]

The Harrison children, Hermione and Thomas, grew up on the farm, as did Isabelle and Elizabeth who were born there in 1752 and 1759.[10] From all accounts they were carefully and thoroughly trained by their parents in the formal manner of the day. Among their father's books were "Nelson on Education" and "Some Thoughts on Education" by the celebrated Mr. John Locke. From the latter he doubtless drew the moral that tutors were to be preferred to schools and that in addition to the usual studies of reading,

Grey Cooper, April 10, 1778, in A. O. 13: Bundle 41; also Bundle 68; and *Bowdoin and Temple Papers*, I, 73.

8. These crops represent what Harrison raised in 1774 when the farm was fully developed, but it had been in that condition since the late fifties. From 1776 to 1779 the Hessians killed off 1,000 poultry worth 6s.9d. each, or £333.15.0 sterling. A. O. 12: ff. 395-96; A. O. 13: Bundle 41.

9. The houses at Newport were small dwellings such as artisans would occupy, the lot being valued at £2,000 sterling. A. O. 12: f. 395; A. O. 13: Bundle 68.

10. Isabelle was baptised on November 26, 1752; Elizabeth on April 25, 1759. Arnold, *Vital Records of Rhode Island*, X, 504; Family Tree, Van Buren Papers.

writing, and cyphering, such embellishments as geography, history, and drawing should be taught. In his library were histories and geographies aplenty, the "Youth's faithful Monitor," "Puerilia," and several other texts suitable for the instruction of youth. Mr. Harrison must have noted with satisfaction Locke's insistence that every gentleman's son should develop a manual skill as a hobby, if for no other reason. Accordingly, Thomas Harrison's talent for drawing received his father's warm encouragement. In later years the Reverend Samuel Peters was to assert (under oath) that Hermione Harrison's "Character and Conduct never tarnished the Instructions and Example of an Excellent Father." Valuing a well-rounded training and never happier than when working among his books, this gentleman saw to it that "all his Children were brought up, in a genteel Stile, and had the best education that the Country could afford." [11]

Although the vagaries of his early life appeared to mark him as a man of the world, Peter Harrison's character rounded out and his talents matured amid the quiet surroundings of his home and family. In him the life of action and that of contemplation were finely blended. He never lost his Quaker seriousness or his addiction to hard work, whether it were in his counting house, for the public service, on the farm, or with one of his favorite diversions. From early youth he had not only been trained to the manual trades, as Locke had advocated, but he had developed his several gifts by means of his hands. Throughout his life he was to keep himself busy with those same hands, and it is noteworthy that prominent among his effects when he died in 1775 were a hand-saw, five augers, eight gimlets, four chisels, a gouge, two draw-shaves, several "plains and Irons," hammers and hatchets—cherished tools of his woodcarving days—and that in one of his bookcases were

11. Testimony of the Rev. Samuel Peters, March 22, 1784, and of John Chandler, April 24, 1784, A. O. 13: Bundle 41.

found such manuals as "Jones' Iron Work," the "Surveyor's Desire fulfilled," "Lane's Surveying," and the "Compleat Shipwright." [12]

Mind and eye were trained as well as hand, and all three were beautifully coordinated. At Harrison Farm was assembled one of New England's finest libraries, a collection that reflected the manifold interests of the owner. For Peter Harrison his library was a place to work, not merely a retreat for leisure and idle enjoyment. Its contents consisted largely of works of reference and instruction, as indeed did those of so many men of the eighteenth century, although, since the books conformed to the bent of the owner, this collection was better rounded than most. Here among his books and manuals he planned and drew the designs of the buildings that today are his monument. He turned to his quartos and folios for information, but this, once acquired, was always fused with his experience and tempered by his rare good judgment. Harrison was well-informed, thorough, and usually alive to current developments in each of the activities he chose to follow; books were the means by which his curiosity about the doings of the Old World was satisfied in the New.

The precision we observe and admire in Harrison's architecture was reflected in his person and demeanor. Nathaniel Smibert's honest brush depicted a pale, rather prim gentleman, proud and sensitive yet mild withal. Peter Harrison was honest, sincere, and dependable, and seems always to have understood the fitness of things. Though always affable and generally well-liked, he was nevertheless reserved. Unlike so many of his friends he was not a joiner. For obvious practical reasons he became a member of the Fire Club, but although he possessed and probably read the "Freemason's Constitution," he never donned the apron.[13] In a

12. Inventory, Appendix B.
13. See Figure 4. There is a list of the members of the Fire Club in the *Rhode Island Historical Magazine*, 5 (1885), 76-77.

quiet, inoffensive way, Harrison refrained from affiliating with anyone outside his little circle without antagonizing his fellow-townsmen. His English birth facilitated this standing apart, for prominent Newporters who, like Ezra Stiles, had been born in the colonies, looked upon him as a "European." In New England he was always something of an exotic, an "English Gentleman," as the Reverend Mr. Burnaby observed.

The basic explanation of Peter Harrison is that having won a place in the colonial gentry he sought to emulate in Rhode Island the life of the eighteenth-century aristocrats he had known in Yorkshire and Nottinghamshire. All Newport considered the Harrison family as definitely of "the better sort"; its master a "Man of Taste." Conservative in politics as in temperament, an admirer of all things British, he mightily respected property with all its appurtenances, its duties and its rights, including the right divine of gentlemen to do as they thought best. As a leading representative of the gentry he always willingly laid aside his dearest projects when church or colony called. This was his duty. His belief in the responsibility of his class for the public weal was as highly developed as was his judgment in architecture.

High seriousness characterized his every act. One seeks in vain for a trace of that saving sense of humor that enabled his acquaintance, Mr. Franklin of Philadelphia, to gloss over the foibles of mankind and find companionship in members of all classes—better, middling, and inferior. It was indeed a tragedy for men like Peter Harrison, and his brother Joseph, that they never discovered how to take the public pulse. Had they been able to bring themselves to mingle with tradesmen and mechanics at Masonic gatherings, or to traffic with other than Anglican merchants, they might not only have glimpsed the direction the colonies were inexorably taking but might also have come to understand and sympathize with local aspirations. Peter's instincts were aristocratic and ten years spent on the quarter deck only served to buttress them. At Newport he and his family dwelt above and apart in their own way.

In the company of friends of his own choosing Peter Harrison was more than sociable and, doubtless, an engaging host. Like an English squire he preferred to entertain intimates at his own fireside rather than foregather with them at the Library, the lodge, or at one of the tavern clubs with which Newport abounded. Naturally, the most frequent visitors at the farm were Joseph and Eleanor Ridgway Harrison and their two children, Richard Acklam and Elizabeth. In social and political as well as family and business relationships Peter and Joseph were unusually close. The elder brother was always the leader; he was both more of a mixer and more of a schemer than Peter. He it was who made the family connections and turned them to account.

Through him Peter and Elizabeth came more and more to move in a small, exclusive circle of English- and Scottish-born merchants, customs officials, and physicians, to whom a few anti-charter Rhode Islanders also attached. Save a sprinkling of Quakers, the group all worshipped at Trinity Church where, in October, 1745, Peter Harrison was assigned the northern half of pew number nineteen by the Vestry upon the payment of £200 currency.[14] Common political, religious, commercial, and cultural bonds tied these people together, and it was only natural that they should coalesce into a "faction." Profoundly significant is the fact that virtually all of Peter Harrison's friends became Tories when the great decision was made.

Among the architect's cronies were three able lawyers: Francis

14. Captain John Dennis "drew" the other half of the pew. It is probable that Peter Harrison became an Anglican before he married Elizabeth Pelham. George C. Mason, *Annals of Trinity Church, Newport, Rhode Island, 1698-1721* (Newport, 1890), 114.

Honyman, delegate to the Albany Congress of 1754 and later King's Advocate for the Vice-Admiralty Court of Rhode Island; Martin Howard, leader of the anti-charter group and soon to be author of the Halifax pamphlets; and Augustus Johnston, Attorney-General of the Colony, 1757-1766. Merchant princes most frequently included in the social life of the farm were: Metcalf Bowler, trimmer extraordinary; wealthy old Godfrey Malbone and his cultivated sons; Patrick Grant, who often shared ventures in ships with the brothers; the Vernons; and in the 1760's George Rome, able but unpopular collection-agent for several London mercantile houses. Jahleel Brenton of the Vice-Admiralty Court, whose property abutted on the Harrisons', and his associates of the customs service were often guests at the Harrison board. Last, but far from least, were a trio of Scottish physicians. Dr. William Hunter, Edinburgh graduate and Jacobite, came over with his beautiful daughters to practice at Newport in 1752, soon numbering the Harrisons among his patients, and with Doctors James Keith and Thomas Moffatt lent a decidedly "philosophical" tone to the group.

Soon after the Harrison brothers arrived in town in 1739, they were introduced to Dr. Thomas Moffatt, who remained a loyal friend of the family until his death in 1787. Countryman and nephew of the painter Smibert, whose Boston partner was his own brother John Moffatt, the physician was also a close friend of the Newport limner Robert Feke, and later the employer of Gilbert Stuart's father, who operated Moffatt's snuff-mill at Narragansett. He possessed several good paintings, among them Smibert's "Bermuda Group" and a Carracci. A bachelor, something of a philanderer, caustic in speech, superior in manner, and a reader of salacious books, the first librarian of the Redwood never achieved popularity with the generality at Newport, and when news that he favored making the colony a royal province got abroad, he speedily became unacceptable to the populace. But in this coterie of Anglicans and royal officials he was highly regarded, and his practice became lucrative. He "lived in habits of intimacy with Joseph and Peter Harrison" for years, and doted on the latter's children. When Hermione arrived in England a penniless refugee in 1778, he took her into his home, assisted her in filing claims with the government, and at his death left her all his property except his paintings. Gay, witty, single, and fond of children, as well as widely read, a patron of the arts with a scientific turn, what group inclined as were the Harrisons would have failed to welcome this Scot in their homes? [15]

The Harrison mansion was admirably suited for the entertainment of guests. Most of the furnishings had been brought over from England and perhaps pieced out here and there by the superb colonial cabinet-work of the Townsends and Goddards of Newport. Ladies must have exclaimed over the modern "Green China Bed furniture and Bedstead" and "China Easy Chair," as well as the "Check'd Draw Curtains" and "Gilt shell Looking Glass with Sconces" in Elizabeth Harrison's chamber. Throughout the house hung twenty-nine pictures, twelve of them neatly "fram'd and Glaz'd," but the attention of connoisseurs immediately focused

15. Among prominent Newport acquaintances of Peter Harrison were: the Reverend Ezra Stiles, Dr. John Brett, Sheriff Walter Chaloner, Abraham Redwood, Samuel Rhodes, Henry Collins, Isaac Stelle, and Speaker Peter Bours of the Rhode Island Assembly.

In Massachusetts he knew some of the Episcopalian gentry very well: Charles Paxton, Sir Henry Frankland, Charles Apthorp, John Powell, John Rowe, Henry Lloyd, and Robert Auchmuty of King's Chapel, Boston; and out at Cambridge Henry and William Vassall, Gilbert Deblois, Robert Hallowell, George Erving, Stephen Greenleaf, Ralph Inman, and their friend Isaac Royall of Medford. These people all became Tories.

For Dr. Moffatt, see his testimony to the Loyalist Commissioners and Joseph Harrison's letter to Sir Grey Cooper, A. O. 13: Bundle 41; *Gentleman's Magazine* (1787), 277-78; Carl Bridenbaugh, ed., *Gentleman's Progress: The Itinerarium of Dr. Alexander Hamilton, 1744* (Chapel Hill, 1948), 102-3, 150-53, 155-56, 158.

on three in particular: a "Large roman painting"; and two "Full length Pictures, one the Crucifixion of our Saviour on the Cross, and the other St. Francis—both Spanish Paintings Valued at 100 Guineas." One would give much to know the provenience of this Catholic art that the erstwhile Quaker acquired when a Spanish prize was condemned at Newport.[16]

Given the taste of the age, it is probable that most frequenters of the Harrison mansion expressed a preference for the likenesses of their hosts that hung in the house after 1756. (Figures 4-5) Like all members of the gentry Peter and Elizabeth wanted their portraits executed, and their friend Dr. Thomas Moffatt arranged for them to sit for his nephew, Nathaniel Smibert, who at twenty-two displayed considerable talent as a painter.[17]

16. When Mrs. Hermione Cargey, Peter's daughter, presented her claims for losses in 1784, she described these paintings as above. James Curgewen, who succeeded Harrison as collector at New Haven, in a deposition of 1822, recollected that they were Italian paintings brought in a prize ship to New Haven. Since peace obtained during Harrison's residence in Connecticut, 1766-1775, I believe that during the French and Indian War a prize was brought into Newport with Spanish paintings in its cargo, although it is just possible they were brought in during King George's War, 1744-1748, when Rhode Island privateers took several Spanish vessels. The other framed pictures, mentioned in the Inventory, Appendix D, were valued at £1.1.0 each. The Particulars lost at Newhaven, etc., A. O. 13: Bundle 41; Deposition of James Curgewen, 1822, Van Buren Papers.

17. Mr. Maurice P. Van Buren of New York owns the original paintings, and the Redwood Library has two inferior copies. John Smibert, father of Nathaniel, is usually thought to have taken the portraits, but a recent examination of the paintings and other evidence by the Reverend Henry Wilder Foote, leading authority on John Smibert, has convinced him and the author that Nathaniel Smibert was the real painter. The manner is the son's, Peter Harrison's clothing is too late for the father's last years of work in the late forties, and a lost letter in the Van Buren Papers, dated July 29, 1756, was from Nathaniel Smibert to Peter Harrison. Family tradition always ascribed the paintings to "Smibert" without specifying which one. The letter mentioned above is probably the one Mr. Shipley Jones, then custodian of the family papers, had in mind on April 20, 1911, when he told Samuel F. Batchelder that the family had at one time possessed a letter describing Peter Harrison's sitting for Smibert. Henry Wilder Foote to author, January 8, 1949; Batchelder Papers, deposited by the Cambridge Historical Society in the Widener Library at Harvard University.

But the proudest possession of the master was his "large and elegant Library of Books, containing . . . between Six and Seven Hundred Volumes, besides Manuscripts and a large Collection of [his] Drawings."   As previously mentioned in these pages, this collection consisted largely of volumes dealing with the several activities of its owner; it was an unusually personalized library. There were, of course, a few works on devotion, a large quarto Bible, "with Cuts and Maps," and an assortment of histories, including one of Spain in Spanish. For the casual reader there were long runs of British periodicals—the *Gentleman's, Universal,* and *London* magazines, the *Spectator* and the *Guardian.* Also representative of contemporary reading tastes were Homer's *Iliad* "in English," Hervey's popular *Meditations,* the inevitable copy of *Hudibras,* Defoe's *Tour Through Great Britain* in four volumes, numerous contemporary plays, *Female Fables,* and *Robinson Crusoe.* Relief from ennui for those not given to reading could always be had by resort to the copy of "Hoyle's Games," or a try at the "Pipe and Tabor" to be found in a corner of the Library.[18]

When Mr. and Mrs. Harrison visited their friends they rode in a curricle drawn by a pair of bays. After a tour of the island on balmy days they occasionally stopped at Timothy Whiting's fashionable tea-house at Middletown where Dean Berkeley had formerly dwelt. Nor is it unlikely that each of the brothers kept a sailboat for pleasure trips on the Bay or excursions to Goat Island where the famous Newport turtle frolics were always held.[19] They were devotees of the fashionable new science and called at Dr. Moffatt's more than once for "learned discourse" about his micro-

18. Testimony of Hermione Cargey, 1785, A. O. 13: Bundle 41; Inventory, Appendices B, C, D.

19. At Boston in 1768, Joseph Harrison had "a Pleasure-Boat, . . . built by himself in a particular and elegant Manner." Seventy-Six Society, *Papers Relating to the Public Events in Massachusetts preceding the American Revolution* (Philadelphia, 1876), 72; Bridenbaugh, "Colonial Newport as a Summer Resort," 18.

scopic experiments and for a view of his "sun microscope," which not only "incredibly magnified" an object upon a movable screen, but as Dr. Hamilton had reported, "afforded a beautiful variety and surprising inter-mixture of colours." [20] These three virtuosi could not have failed to display the greatest curiosity in the lectures on Electricity given at Newport in January, 1752, by Benjamin Franklin's protégé, Ebenezer Kinnersley of Philadelphia, and we may be sure that they presented their playing-card tickets for admission to the Colony House for the series of public lectures on anatomy and surgery, the first ever given in America, delivered by their friend Dr. William Hunter in the years 1754-1756. [21]

These were years of prosperity and domestic felicity for Elizabeth and Peter Harrison. Happiness over the birth of Isabelle, their third child, on November 26, 1752, was soon to be lessened by news of the death of Peter's mother at York, England, on May 4, 1753. [22] The only other event of family import at this time was the opening of King's Chapel for worship on August 21, 1754, although the edifice was far from complete and the plan for the beautiful spire had been discarded. One wonders if the architect made the long overland journey to Boston to view his masterpiece, and whether, perchance, he heard that the adoption of the two tiers of windows had elicited from Boston's incorrigible punster, the Reverend Mather Byles, the uninformed, provincial comment that "he had heard of the canons of the Church but had never seen the portholes before." [23]

During the time that Peter's reputation as a man of quality and consequence was developing, the Harrisons were acquiring

20. *Dr. Hamilton's Itinerarium*, 158.
21. *Boston Evening Post*, Nov. 4, 18, 1751; Jan. 20, 1752; Jan. 20, 27, Feb. 3, 1755; Mason, *Annals of Trinity Church*, 120; Colonial Society of Massachusetts, *Transactions*, 19 (1916-17), 283.
22. Family Tree, Van Buren Papers.
23. *Providence Gazette*, Jan. 28, 1769.

ever increasing distinction as honest and trustworthy merchants. Throughout 1750 life at Newport had proceeded uneventfully on the whole, although to anyone attempting to conduct business on an intercolonial scale, the gyrations of the Rhode Island paper currency must have been maddening. Since 1743 the value of the bills of credit had declined one half; the total of £525,355 reported to be worth £75,111 sterling when issued, was valued at only £35,445 in 1750. Such was the burden of a "complaint" sent home to England in September by seventy-two merchants, including Peter and Joseph Harrison, praying the Crown to forbid the Rhode Island Assembly to issue any more bills and to insist that it recall the issue of the previous August, thereby relieving the petitioners "from the injury and oppression of a flood of fluctuating sinking paper bills of public credit." Passage by Parliament the following year of a law prohibiting the issuance of currency by any of the New England governments was the answer to this and similar petitions.[24]

Most of the Harrisons' business consisted in acting as American agents for Joseph Manesty and Company of Liverpool and Christopher Scott of Hull. With these houses they shared in the ownership of one or more Rhode Island-built vessels. Not only did the brothers import in their ship *American* "a Variety of European Goods, suitable for the Season," from Hull and Liverpool to dispense by wholesale or retail from their Thames Street store, but they supplied people across the Bay in the Narragansett Country with articles ordered by mail.[25] No better testimony of their stand-

24. It is interesting to note that John Banister did not sign the petition. *R. I. Col. Recs.*, V, 283, 311-13; Stock, *Proceedings and Debates of the British Parliament*, V, 448-50, 508-11.

25. Unfortunately none of their commercial correspondence has survived, but some idea of their activities and of the complicated methods of making trans-Atlantic payments in the colonial period may be gained from reading the papers on a series of protested bills of exchange in R. I. Land Evidences, VI, 90, 94, 202, 315. John Lyon of Wilmington, North Carolina, shipped naval stores to Chris-

ing in the business community can be adduced than the willingness of the Quaker merchant Thomas Richardson to apprentice his son William for seven years to Joseph and Peter Harrison, and the fact that when the lad came free of his indentures his father informed Philadelphia Friends that he "is well qualified for Business, and has given them Good Satisfaction in their Service." [26]

In April of 1750 Peter looked after the business while Joseph headed the Rhode Island commission to determine the boundary between that colony and Massachusetts, and he may have assisted with the preparation of the map of the survey that Joseph submitted with the report.[27] From the counting house at his "Store on Thames Street near Captain John Brown's Wharf," Peter Harrison managed the affairs of the partnership. This office was a small, severely furnished place, judged by modern standards, with a desk, a few chairs, a high table at which the apprentice sat on a stool posting ledgers or copying letters in a great leather-bound book, and a box of pigeonholes, each of which contained the papers per-

topher Scott at Hull, and presented sterling bills of exchange to Peter Harrison, who could not honor them since the firm had no sterling money belonging to Scott. All colonial business was conducted on a leisurely basis, and long term credit was accepted as inevitable by merchants. One of the firm's customers, the Reverend James McSparran of St. Paul's, Narragansett, dropped into the store on September 28, 1751, to pay Captain Harrison £45.10s. "for a Piece of black Sagathee he sometime ago sent me." On several occasions, however, the brothers had to go into court to force payment of sums owed to them. Jabez Carpenter, Day Book, 1750-52; and Autograph Receipt Book, 1743-53; John Hadwen, Day Book, 1751-58; Thomas Vernon, Account Book, 1739-72, Newport Historical Society; Daniel Goodwin, ed., *A Letter Book and Abstract of Out Services* (Boston, 1899), 41, 62; Superior Court Records, August Term, 1750; Inferior Court of Common Pleas, Volume D, 548, Newport County Court House.

26. Thomas Richardson to Margaret Bowne and Henry Haywood, May 9, 1759, Thomas Richardson, Letter Book, 98-99; Jabez Carpenter, Receipt Book, 1743-53, unpaged, Newport Historical Society; Newport Historical Society, Autographs, no. 1199.

27. A Map of the Country Adjacent to the North Boundary Line of the Colony of Rhode Island, 1750, photostat from the Public Record Office, London; *R. I. Col. Recs.*, V, 281, 322-25, 333.

taining to the purchase, cargoes, and voyages of a single ship, and other accounts neatly tied up with red tapes—the filing system of the colonial merchant. Because he always sought to inform himself fully about matters in which he was engaged, Mr. Harrison possessed more books on shipping and commerce than most of his fellow-traders. For use at the counting house he not only had such convenient reference works as "Muir's book-keeping," "Aitken's Register," a "Letter-Writer," "the Ship and Supercargo's book Keeper," the "Polite English Secretary," and "Everyman his own Lawyer," but volumes on "Naval Trade and Commerce," "Gordon's Geographical Grammar," a "Description of the Orkneys," and a useful work on "Piracy and Plunder," as well as numerous charts, including two of the Mediterranean and one of the "Welch Coast." [28]

The counting house was no retreat for contemplation, set off as it usually was in one corner of the "Store" or warehouse.[29] Familiar smells of cordage, tar, Narragansett cheese, salt pork, lumber; the musty scent of dry goods; the pungent odor of molasses; and the not infrequent stench of rotting fish permeated the whole establishment at all hours. The place was noisy too. Outside along Thames Street (which rhymes with James) from sunrise to dusk an endless line of carts and wagons passed up and down, their oxen or horses urged on by the cries, oaths, goadings, and whip-crackings of rough carters; here also one heard continually the guttural jabberings of Negro porters, the inevitable barking of countless dogs and all the usual hustle and bustle of a busy waterfront traffic. Within the store and out on the wharf were generated familiar, unmuted sounds by creaking tackle, squealing windlasses, rolling casks, the curses of porters and stevedores. Nor was the Harrison warehouse free from legions of squeaking rats and other vermin common to

28. Inventory, Appendix B.
29. A *store* was a warehouse, in contrast to a *shop* where goods were retailed.

all seaports. Indeed, the romance of "Oldport Days" is largely a fiction born of twentieth-century nostalgia.

Of course, this scene was a familiar one to Peter Harrison, who passed a few hours each day in the counting house, looking over the wharf, and issuing instructions to his apprentice, William Richardson, or to Captains Paul Pease and Field Wilkinson, then sallied forth to "walk on Change" with other local merchants and to learn prices and hear the latest news before he retired to his mansion for a mid-afternoon dinner, quiet, and recreation.

Few colonials of the seventeen-fifties would have denied that "wars must right wrongs which Frenchmen have begun," but to a trading community like Newport the French and Indian War brought grave economic dislocation. The highly vulnerable slave trade was almost snuffed out, coastal trading was curtailed and suffered inroads from French privateers, while commerce with the mother country was safe only under the cumbersome system of naval convoys. Peacetime clandestine traffic with the French sugar islands, where foodstuffs and lumber were exchanged for molasses and coin, became in time of war a "trade with the Enemy," which could be carried on only by sundry devious subterfuges. Herein was no intent of treason; Rhode Islanders thought only of trade. They proudly pointed to the privateers on which they laid out their profits and the ravages these inflicted on French commerce. Newport's survival as a commercial community genuinely depended on illicit trade and privateering. Such was the situation confronting Peter Harrison when Joseph and his family crossed to England in the summer of 1755 on what turned out to be a protracted visit.[30]

30. Like excited people of our own day, Joseph Harrison sailed without remembering that he had not paid for his subscription to the *New York Gazette* since November, 1752. A List for the New York Gazette, what's due to Jany. 1st, 1757, Newport Historical Society.

Peter carried on the business at Newport, "gaining great credit and reputation as a Merchant," without, so far as we know, entering into trade with the enemy or sending out a single privateer. In spite of ruinous insurance rates as high as twenty per cent to twenty-eight per cent, and the shortage of hands for merchant ships caused by the lure of high wages and prize shares on privateersmen, he appears to have confined his activities to coasting and the business with London, Liverpool, and Hull he had built up during the years of peace. In this his decisions were wise. Profits were smaller, but so were losses. And Peter Harrison did not so poignantly share the gloom of his privateering friends, Metcalf Bowler, Godfrey Malbone, Henry Collins and the rest, over the loss of between ninety and one hundred of the vessels owned at Newport in the one year 1758.[31]

It may have been the uncertainty of normal commercial transactions during the French and Indian War or expectation of profits in a new line that led Peter Harrison to purchase a whaling vessel, but at any rate he had done so by March, 1755, if not earlier. This was one of the earliest, possibly the first whaler, out of Newport; Harrison may have ventured in this line because of his familiarity with the whale fishery at Hull in his youth. The sloop *Success*, Captain Joseph Jenkins, got hard usage and needed frequent repairs to her chimney; in January, 1760, a new "Cobuse" or shack had to be erected on deck for trying out blubber and head-matter. The investment was profitable since the oil and head-matter were sold

31. James Honyman, Newport deputy, told the Rhode Island Assembly on June 11, 1759, that "the merchants of the town of Newport, have lost in the course of their trade, upwards of two millions of money [in pounds] since the commencement of the present war." William P. Sheffield, *The Privateersmen of Newport* (Newport, 1883), 27-29, 52-55; Henry to Samuel Ward, February 19, 1758, Ward Papers, Box 1, Rhode Island Historical Society; Bruce M. Bigelow, Commerce between Rhode Island and the West Indies before the Revolution, Pt. I, Chap. VI, 25-75, Thesis, Brown University Library; *R. I. Col. Recs.*, VI, 212.

directly to the several spermaceti-candle "manufactories" located at Newport.[32]

When James Franklin established the *Newport Mercury* in June, 1758, local merchants hastened to advertise their wares in its columns. For over a year the Harrisons held back, probably because as agents they had nothing to sell; but with the collapse of French power trading prospects brightened, and on October 9, 1759, the *Mercury* earned their rather laconic notice:

> Just Imported
> and to be Sold by
> Joseph & Peter Harrison
> At their Store near the Wharf
> of Capt. John Brown
> A Variety of European Goods Suitable for the Season

This advertisement of the goods Joseph had shipped over ran in the newspaper through October. In January, 1760, a somewhat similar one announced various European articles "just imported."[33]

In the wake of the war came the inevitable economic crisis, and many Newport merchants who, like Henry Collins, had overinvested in privateering were ruined. Times proved bad for all, and the meager evidence available suggests that things were not going very well for the Harrisons either. On John Banister's books as late as 1759 the brothers were posted as owing him £2,549, and Peter was down for an additional £360.8.2, as his third of a debt Elizabeth had contracted in 1742.[34] In 1761 Joseph Cowley sued his brother-in-law Peter Harrison in an action of detinue in the Court of Common Pleas for allegedly withholding from him

32. A Robert Jenkins made spermaceti candles in 1761. *Commerce of Rhode Island*, I, 92, 130 ff.; copy of a mason's account in Samuel F. Batchelder Papers, Cambridge Historical Society; John Hadwen, Letter Book, under June 2, 1753; October 5, 1754; March 26, 1755.

33. *Newport Mercury*, Oct. 9, 16, 30, 1759; Jan. 1, 1760.

34. Banister Account Book, 1739-58, p. 6; Letter Book, 1761, p. 76.

"sundry sorts of goods, plate, jewels, etc." When Harrison pleaded somewhat speciously that the sheriff had not specified "the particular goods, plate and jewels," the Court abated the action on this technicality and awarded him the costs of £7.17.0.[35] Cowley did not bring suit again.

Nor was the indebtedness kept within the family. The mason who built the caboose and chimneys for the *Success*, as well as a new "Celler Wall" for Peter, was still owed £107.5.10 currency in 1762. On the other hand Hadwen and Thurston were promptly paid for stationery. Partly because of the habits of the time and partly because of the drastic shortage of money, payments by the brothers were slow. They had as yet made no reduction of their loan of £4,000 from John Freebody which fell due in 1750, although the interest was paid regularly. (Figure 9) In 1769, four years after Peter had moved away from the town, the firm of "Joseph and Peter Harrison" appeared on the list of "Bad Debts" due their old acquaintance, the bankrupt William Richardson, for the sum of £1,108.2.3 currency. Some solace could be derived from good company, for the names of John Goddard, Augustus Johnston, Benjamin Bagnall, Jr., Dr. Silvester Gardiner, and Samuel Brenton were also there.[36]

Eighteenth-century business practices must never be measured by twentieth-century standards. Nothing can be more misleading. Every colonial merchant was sorely beset by the difficulty of making cash returns for the goods he purchased from England, and consequently nearly everyone, usually because of events beyond his control, fell behind in his payments. In 1762 William Stead of London dunned Christopher Champlin of Newport for payment

---

35. Inferior Court of Common Pleas, Volume F, 487.

36. Hadwen and Thurston, Day Book, 1751-58, p. 748; Newport Historical Society, Autographs, no. 1199; Batchelder, Peter Harrison, 68; Petitions to the General Assembly, XIII, 36, Rhode Island Archives.

on goods "sent you ... charg'd at 12 Months' Credit, which is now upwards of 3 years' standing." [37] Within the colony so great was the effect of the draining of specie to England that settlements of local obligations were not infrequently postponed for years.

Whether the Harrisons were any more dilatory in paying their debts than their mercantile colleagues cannot be determined because of the destruction of their papers. And besides, there is the pertinent question of how much was owed to them—and for how long? This much is certain, they did not fail in trade; instead they made an honorable withdrawal when opportunities arose, as later pages will show. Times were never the same at Newport after the last French War. For many years trade did not resume its flow into "the old Channel of Regularity," and the brothers concurred with Henry Cruger's remark that of "late all seems to have been floating on an Ocean of Scepticism." [38]

As a former mariner, a merchant, and an architect Peter Harrison was throughout his residence at Newport concerned with Beavertail Light on Conanicut Island. In 1749 Joseph had served on the colony committee to superintend the erection of the structure, of which his friend Dr. William Douglass wrote the following description: "The Diameter at the Base is 24 Feet, and at the Top 13 Feet. The Height from the Ground to the Top of the Cornice is 58 Feet, round which is a Gallery, and within that stands the Lanthorn, which is about 11 Feet high, and 8 Feet Diameter." The third lighthouse to be built in America, it was unfortunately of timber construction and on July 23, 1753, only three days after the General Treasurer had paid Joseph and Peter Harrison's bill

37. *Commerce of Rhode Island*, I, 93.
38. Cruger to Aaron Lopez, March 1, 1766, *Commerce of Rhode Island*, I, 145, 189.

of £329.7.4 for paint, the building burned to the ground.[39] At its August session the Rhode Island Assembly made provision for the immediate erection of a new and more substantial lighthouse and authorized the building committee to use "all of the stone and brick at Fort George." [40]

The new lighthouse and a dwelling for the keeper were designed by Peter Harrison. As one learns to expect of eighteenth-century buildings, they were slowly constructed, and temporary beacons were still in use as late as August, 1754, when the Assembly empowered the Treasurer "to hire" £4,000 currency to pay for the structures. The delay arose in part from difficulties in purchasing two acres of land from Josiah Arnold, but sometime before May, 1755, the lighthouse was completed at a cost of nearly £500 more than had originally been authorized. On "A Plan of the Town and Harbour of Newport on Rhode Island," which he drew in 1755 (Figure 11), Harrison carefully sketched in his lighthouse—a tower of three stories, cornice, gallery, and lantern—but he did not include the keeper's house which was not finished until early the following year.

Yet this did not end Harrison's connection with Beavertail. In February, 1756, he was placed on a committee "to put the Light House into good repair." In addition to the annoyance of keeper-trouble, the authorities found the illumination inadequate. Peter Harrison served in June, 1761, on another committee which sent Josiah Arnold to Massachusetts to procure a model of the "lan-

39. The earlier lights were erected at Boston, 1716, and Brant's Point, Nantucket, 1746. Colonial Records of Rhode Island, VI, 147, 324; Douglass, *Summary*, II, 98; William G. Low, "A Short History of the Beaver Tail Light, Conanicut, Rhode Island," Jamestown Historical Society, *Bulletin*, No. 7 (1936), 9; *R. I. Col. Recs.*, V, 372; *Pennsylvania Gazette*, Aug. 2, 1753. The *Newport Mercury* of Oct. 15, 1825, prints the bearings from Beavertail Light as taken by Captain Joseph Harrison and William Paul, Oct. 7, 1753.

40. *R. I. Col. Recs.*, V, 372.

thorn" of Boston light; in the following year he was among those authorized to change the lighting gear at Beavertail.[41]

Contrary to accepted beliefs, war played a most significant part in the lives of the American colonists. Peter Harrison's first nine years in Rhode Island, 1739-1748, were all spent under wartime conditions, and he was, as we have seen, captured at sea. During his last voyage his wife lived in constant fear that he might be again taken. Although he probably did not know it, the attack of Charles Langlade and his Ottawa allies on the English fur traders' post at Pickawillany in the distant Ohio Country on July 21, 1752, began the world war which marked a turning point in the fortunes of the House of Harrison and once again drew Peter back into the public service.

Fort George, on Goat Island, which he had planned in 1745, had been allowed to fall into decay by the colony. There was the customary sad story of British and colonial neglect extending even to the armament: "within the battery, viz: twenty-four cannon and twenty-four carriages, chiefly broke," reported Captain William Mumford.[42] It is nevertheless greatly to the credit of the General Assembly that in the summer of 1754, almost a year before Braddock's stunning disaster at Monongahela, it voted to raise £5,000 old tenor by taxation for repairing the fort. So ruinous did the works prove that shortly an additional £5,000 had to be allocated, and James Sheffield and William Reed, two Newport deputies, were selected to oversee the repairs at Goat Island.[43]

Grimly realizing their helpless position should French ships attack Newport, the inhabitants resolved at a town meeting on January 29, 1755, to do something at the expense of the town "in

41. *R. I. Col. Recs.*, V, 372, 384, 393, 395, 402, 432, 483-84, 516; and, more fully, Lighthouse Accounts, Rhode Island Archives.

42. *R. I. Col. Recs.*, V, 387.

43. *Ibid.*, 393, 398, 399, 401-2.

addition to what the General Assembly have [ordered] to be done toward the repair of Fort George." They voted to assess an emergency tax of £5,000 old tenor, providing that anyone might work out his share at the fort, and chose a committee of twelve, among whom were both Harrisons, "to be at Fort George to advise" with Sheffield and Reed about "what may be proper to be done." [44]

Soon it became evident that more repairs would not insure the safety of Newport, but rather that the works must be dismantled, redesigned, and rebuilt. Because of his great knowledge of military engineering and his known willingness to serve, Peter Harrison was soon shouldering the heaviest responsibility of anyone on the committee. Just as in 1738, and again in 1745, the General Assembly hoped that the ordnance for the new fort would be supplied "from home," and in February it ordered a letter drafted to that effect to accompany a plan of the works. To Peter, therefore, went the task of not only designing the fortifications but drawing two additional sets of plans, which were sent to London in March, 1755, to indicate the extent of the "repairs and enlargements." [45]

In planning the new fortifications Harrison relied heavily on the studies of the eminent John Muller, German-born headmaster of the Royal Military Academy at Woolwich, who published a series of authoritative volumes on military science and engineering. Especially did his *Treatise of the Elementary Part of Fortifications, Regular and Irregular* (London, 1746, 1761) serve to teach English readers the intricacies of the designs of Vauban and other Continental engineers and also to provide a convenient glossary of the terms used by military engineers. Peter owned this volume, Muller's *Attack and Defense of Fortified Places*, Muller's book on artillery, and also the works of the acknowledged master of defen-

44. Newport Town Meeting Records, 1741-76, II, 124.
45. *R. I. Col. Recs.*, V, 409; C. O. 5: 16, 163, Library of Congress Transcripts.

sive warfare, Sebastien Le Prestre de Vauban, and his countryman, Guillaume Le Blond.[46]

The passion for symmetry and regularity everywhere so evident in the seventeenth and eighteenth centuries could not fail to infect the military architects. Gentlemen found laid down in Muller's treatises the classical rules for erecting fortifications just as they discovered similar principles of architecture set forth by Palladio and in the books of Gibbs and Kent. And yet, Muller's prime contribution in his volume on fortifications was to emphasize that "particular care should be taken, in tracing plans on paper, in order to know whether they are practicable or not; which has been neglected by many, even some of those who are generally esteemed the best writers." [47]

As he puzzled over the best way to fortify Goat Island's jagged shoreline, Peter Harrison agreed with Muller that "the true art consists in making irregular fortifications everywhere equally strong." Notwithstanding his earlier admiration for M. Coehorn's defenses at Bergen-op-Zoom, in 1755 he followed Muller's advice and concentrated more on the style of Vauban, who "always made the exterior side next to a river much longer than any other." And like Muller he readily perceived that for English and colonial purposes "particular notice" had to be given to the construction of works near water to protect the maritime strength of "this nation on account of the many forts we have and daily build." [48]

The plans of Fort George were ready by March, 1755, and two carefully drawn copies labelled "A Plan and Profile of the Fortifi-

46. See Harrison's inventory, Appendix B. In 1757 John Muller published at London *A System of Mathematicks, Fortifications and Artillery*, in six volumes (actually volumes five and six are bound together), a set of which I have consulted at the Mariner's Museum. Harrison had single volumes, not the set, including *The Attack and Defense of Fortified Places* which was not included in the collected works.

47. Muller, *System*, III, v.

48. *Ibid.*, vi-vii, x, xi, 144-45, 169, 171, 172.

cations now erecting to defend the Town and Harbour of Newport on Rhode Island" were dispatched to the Board of Trade.
(Figure 10) In these we see the same talent Harrison displayed
in his civil architecture. Borrowing methods, forms, and details
from the best manuals available, he combined them with his own
ideas and experience in producing an "irregular fortification" at
Goat Island of which John Muller, himself, might have been
proud. There was in these works no pale copy of something taken
from Vauban or Coehorn, but instead a skillful adaptation of classic
elements in the solution of a practical problem. Peter Harrison was
maturing as an architect and an engineer, and he turned to the
books in this instance much as a professional would today. Above
all, he was too sensible to sacrifice the defense of his home and
community on the altar of eighteenth-century symmetry.[49] Three
copies of his plans exist: the two he made early in 1755; and a third
finished in October, 1756. All of them, but especially the latter
(Figure 10), reveal a skill in draftsmanship, unique in English
America, that well merited the adjective "handsome" applied to
them by the General Assembly.[50]

To plan and design an intricate set of defensive works was one
thing; to carry them to completion was another. In a petition to
Sir Thomas Robinson, His Majesty's Secretary of State, written
in April, 1755, requesting twenty more cannon, Governor Stephen
Hopkins mentioned that "great Numbers of People are now daily
at Work in making the . . . repair and Enlargements." Actually the
work progressed with incredible slowness, impeded no doubt by

49. Muller, "A Treatise on the Elementary Part of Fortification," *System*, III,
18-66, 144-45, 146, 172, 218-40, and particularly, Plates 3 (construction of counter-
guards), 7 (construction of "Profils"), 32 (forts and redoubts); Muller, "A Treatise containing the Practical Parts of Fortification," *System*, IV, Section IV, 130-36,
and Plates 6 ("How to make the Plan"), 7 ("How to trace the Plan of a Fortress
on the Ground").

50. The two copies dated 1755 are in the Public Record Office; the third is
in the Henry E. Huntington Library at San Marino, California.

the uncertainty of any gift of ordnance from England. The colony agent, Richard Partridge, sent one of Harrison's "Profils" around London offices without much success. Meanwhile, in December, the General Assembly of Rhode Island appointed a Newport deputy, Peter Bours, and Captain Peter Harrison "a committee to prepare a plan of the harbor of Newport, and a profile of Fort George; . . . together with the returns of the number of inhabitants, small arms, etc." that would be needed, and directed that these be promptly forwarded to Sir Thomas Robinson.[51]

Turning from engineering to cartography, Peter Harrison supplied the Assembly with "A Plan of the Town and Harbour of Newport on Rhode Island" (Figure 11) before the close of 1756. Fruit of years of experience by an expert practical navigator who was at the same time an accomplished draftsman, this accurate and neatly embellished map clearly places its maker in the front rank of early American cartographers and entitles him to share laurels with Captain Cyprian Southack, Walter Hoxton, and Joshua Fisher as pioneer hydrographers. Save that his soundings are too shoal, Harrison's chart is complete and accurate enough in its topography for use today.[52] Following directions from the General Assembly he "put marks upon such places" as he judged "necessary to be fortified," designating them by the accepted method of the time as A (Rose Island), and B (the point where

51. In the Huntington Library is a "List of Cannon and Mortars necessary for the Fortifications Erecting to defend the Town and Harbour of Newport on Rhode Island," in a hand strongly resembling Harrison's. According to this there were at the fort six twenty-four-pounders and eighteen eighteen-pounders; "wanting" were twelve thirty-two- or forty-two-pounders, fifty-four twenty-four-pounders, thirty small cannon "for the Flanks," and six mortars. C. O. 5: 16, 163, 165; *R. I. Col. Recs.*, V, 441-42, 469-70, 521-22; Kimball, *Correspondence*, II, 156.

52. It should be noted, however, that Harrison's soundings are about the same as those on the map of Narragansett Bay in the *Atlantic Neptune*, and probably were not too shoal for the time the map was made. The original map is in the Public Record Office.

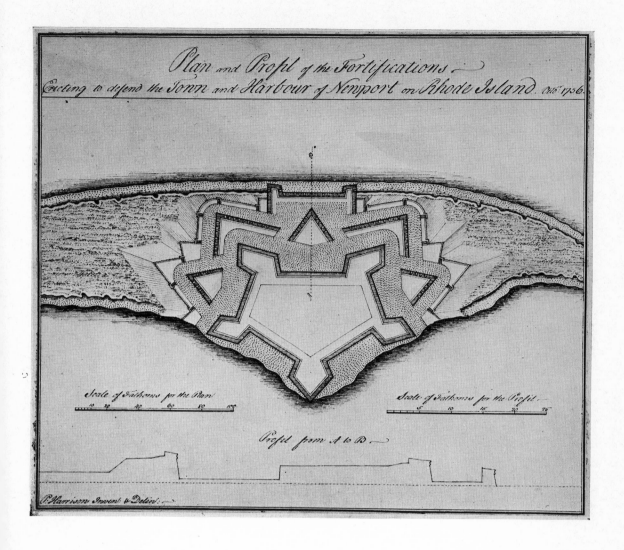

FIGURE 10. One of the three drawings of Fort George and Goat Island which, taken with the map of Newport (Figure 11), clearly demonstrate Peter Harrison's skill as a draughtsman. *Courtesy of the Henry E. Huntington Library*

FIGURE 11. A Plan of the Town and Harbour of Newport on Rhode Island, drawn by Peter Harrison in 1755. *Public Record Office, London*

Fort Adams now stands). No better positions for batteries could have been chosen. Prominently displayed on the "Plan" were Harrison's new lighthouse on "Bever Tail" and the projected works at Fort George. Unlike other cartographers Harrison never had his chart engraved and published, but with it and the more detailed plans of the fortifications he supplied the English authorities with every single bit of information pertaining to the defenses of lower Narragansett Bay.

Not until January 10, 1757, did the General Assembly of Rhode Island and Providence Plantations direct the speaker and Peter Bours "to wait on Captain Peter Harrison and render him the thanks of this government for all the favors they have received from him; and in particular the two plans of the Fort." But even this belated gesture was almost nullified by a request "to lend another of said plans unto the Commissioners appointed to wait on his Excellency the Earl of Loudoun at the Congress in Boston." [53]

Very little progress was made with work on the fortifications, despite elaborate plans, repeated legislation, and dire need. One obstacle may very well have been materials, for in February, 1756, permission was granted "to make use of the stones in the old Fort towards building the new one." Another was the vast expense the project entailed; in August resort was had to a lottery. Labor was scarce as always in colonial days, and one questions how hard the soldiers at the Fort labored at the works when they were not on guard duty. Only £3,103.9.5½ of the £15,000 earmarked for the fortifications had been expended by September, 1756, when the Assembly, noting that "they remain unfinished," resolved that it was "absolutely necessary that said works should continue." [54]

Even more concerned, the Newport Town Meeting instructed

53. *R. I. Col. Recs.*, VI, 13.

54. And yet in October all the soldiers at Fort George were ordered discharged and the powder removed to the Newport magazine. *Ibid.*, V, 483, 505, 511, 514, 543.

its committee on the fort, which of course included Peter Harrison, in April, 1758, to lend Captain William Mumford "all proper assistance for the expediting the said works in the best manner." To the June meeting the committee reported:

> We having been over at Goat Island and visited sd. works do give it as our opinion that the Marlons [yet] unfinished in the North and South Countergard be formed on their proper forms with timber, either red cedar, pine or oak, squared at the ends, [and that] the same be strongly put together by Duftailing or Trunowling, after which we advise they should be filled with earth out of the ditch as used for the fortifying and strengthening the works. It is also our opinion that as the magazine is much decayed and rotten there be a proper Magazine forth with prepared for the reception of powder, &c., and that all sorts of materials necessary for the fighting the guns already mounted be speedily prepared and lodged in the Fort. We also further advise that the Ravelin which is not yet [joined] to the North Countergard be finished with all possible expedition.[55]

Eleven months later the General Assembly voted to pay £10,000 from the Treasury to procure stores for the Fort, "for completing the ravelins," and for enlisting six men to labor on the works. Upon Newport they shifted the responsibility of "laying out the money," and upon a new town committee, including Peter Harrison, fell the burden of the actual work.[56] All construction was dropped with alacrity with the fall of Quebec.[57]

At London throughout the war Richard Partridge patiently, though doggedly, pressed the authorities to grant the guns and equipment needed "to render the Fortification compleat." He repeatedly emphasized the heavy expenditures the colony had undergone, pointing out with the use of Peter Harrison's survey

55. Newport Town Records, II, 156, 166.
56. *R. I. Col. Recs.*, VI, 208-9; Newport Town Meeting Records, V, 169.
57. From the accounts in the volume marked "French Wars (Ft. George)" in the Rhode Island Archives one gathers the impression that no extensive work was undertaken at Fort George after 1756.

that Newport Harbor, "perhaps the finest in America," was so deep that "the largest Ship may anchor within 200 yards of the Shoar," and that consequently the town needed adequate defenses. But in October, 1759, he had to confess to Governor Greene that all his efforts had been in vain. He had even petitioned the King-in-Council, "wherein I had the assistance of Captain Joseph Harrison," then in England, "and besides, he was so kind as to use his Interest with some eminent Persons about it." Peter also reported that Joseph was pushing the petition "under the Direction and with the Assistance of the Earl of Halifax." [58]

As hostilities stopped the project came to nothing. Construction at Fort George was never carried far enough to warrant its inclusion in Mary Ann Rocque's *A Set of Plans and Forts in America, reduced from Actual Surveys* (London, 1763), although Peter Harrison had developed one of the best and most elaborate designs.[59] The portion actually built is clearly delineated on the excellent plan of Newport made for the British Army by Charles Blaskowitz in 1777.

58. Kimball, *Correspondence*, II, 209-10, 211-12, 258-59, 262-65; Henry to Samuel Ward, Feb. 19, 1758, Ward Papers, Box 1, Rhode Island Historical Society.
59. A copy is in the John Carter Brown Library.

IV

A Masterly Architect

THE year of Wolfe's victory at Quebec also ushered in the supreme achievement in American colonial architecture. Between March, 1759, and July, 1760, occurred Peter Harrison's second and more important burst of architectural activity: one which produced in rapid succession plans for the Jewish Synagogue, the Freemason's Hall, and the Brick Market at Newport, as well as those of Christ Church at Cambridge in Massachusetts.

The tiny group of fifteen or twenty families of Sephardic Jews who composed the Congregation Jeshuat Israel decided early in 1759 to erect a synagogue at Newport.[1] They wrote to their brethren of Shearith Israel at New York in March that they had just purchased for £1,500 old tenor a small lot on Griffin (now Touro) Street, measuring ninety feet in front and one hundred sixteen in depth, which they had placed under the trusteeship of a building committee consisting of Jacob Rodriguez Rivera, Moses Levy, and Isaac Hart. Financial support for this shoestring undertaking soon came from Sephardic groups at New York, Jamaica, Curaçao, Surinam, London, and Amsterdam.[2] The members of

1. Although there were some Ashkenazim (or Eastern European Jews) in the Congregation the Sephardic (or Portuguese) ritual was used exclusively. *Literary Diary of Ezra Stiles*, I, 11*n.*

2. American Jewish Historical Society, *Publications*, 27 (1920), 181, 408; Newport Land Evidences, XIV, 412, 433; XV, 376, City Hall, Newport. The most

the building committee were all merchants with stores on Thames Street, and Levy and Rivera were members of the Redwood Library.[3] Although circumscribed by meager funds, these men of taste desired a handsome building for their temple and quite naturally turned to their gifted fellow-townsman for a design. Peter Harrison readily accommodated them.

Working rapidly he produced designs in time for work on the new edifice to begin in August. That he approached this task with the greatest zest can scarcely be questioned, for it offered an unusual challenge. Consider the problem! Wedded as he was to the neo-Palladian style, how could he design a building after the sets of classical plans with which he was familiar, and at the same time suit it to the oriental spirit of the Hebrew faith and ritual? Though the two propositions seem irreconcilable, in Peter Harrison's hands the solution was simple, logical, and ingenious.

From the Reverend Isaac Touro, youthful Chuzzan recently arrived from study at the Rabbinical Academy in Amsterdam, the architect received instruction in the approved lay-out of a Spanish-Portuguese synagogue.[4] It is also barely possible he may have viewed that of Amsterdam during a visit to the Low Countries in 1744. (Figure 31) Whatever the source, the similarity of the interiors of the Dutch and Rhode Island temples is so striking as to confirm the belief that he was acquainted with the plan of the Dutch building.[5]

---

recent and most accurate account of the Synagogue is by Lee M. Friedman, "The Newport Synagogue," *Old Time New England*, 36 (1946), 49-57; Morris A. Gutstein, *The Story of the Jews of Newport* (New York, 1936), though more detailed is uncritical and less reliable.

3. Mason, *Annals of the Redwood Library*, 34, 37-38, 47.

4. Morris A. Gutstein, *Aaron Lopez and Judah Touro* (New York, 1939), 66; Gutstein, *Jews of Newport*, 72, 93-94.

5. English interest in synagogue architecture resulted in publication of an interior view of that of Amsterdam in the *Gentleman's Magazine*, 1778, p. 200. See Figure 31.

The all-important feature of the Newport Synagogue is its plan. Armed with a knowledge of what was wanted, Harrison turned to his library for an inspiration. As he flipped the pages of his various books of architecture he was on the lookout for ideas for the Ark, the reading desk, and the galleries for the women of the congregation, but always the familiar church of the Anglican ritual was foremost in his mind. For a general plan of the interior he seems to have been influenced by a plate in Kent's *Designs of Inigo Jones*. This was a design for an arched, two-story, galleried hall at Whitehall Palace, having Corinthian columns superposed upon Ionic. (Figure 32) Most of the necessary details for the interior colonnades can be found in Kent, except for the curved frieze, which he may have selected from the *Rules for Drawing* by James Gibbs. (Figure 30) In the same work are prototypes for the gallery balustrade and also the models for the exterior porch (Figures 28-29) and the consoles for the interior of the doorway. It must be emphasized, nevertheless, that Harrison possessed nearly all of the currently used architectural books and manuals, and that one cannot determine with certainty precisely from which books his sources derive.[6]

When he came to the Ark he found himself in a genuine predicament. No such thing had ever been designed either for a Christian church or for a pagan temple. Here his imagination rose to the occasion and he achieved a magnificent solution by adapting for the lower part, the Ark proper, a design for a Tuscan altarpiece that he had previously used for the altar of King's Chapel and which is found in Batty Langley's *Treasury of Designs;* above it he placed an ornamental frame which appears to be a fusion of one of Kent's drawings with another taken from the *Designs of Inigo*

6. Kent, *Designs of Inigo Jones*, Plates 35, 50; Gibbs, *Rules for Drawing*, Plates 39, 41, 47.

Jones and others by Isaac Ware.[7] (Figures 33-35) The finished design, however, was substantially modified by his own notions of what the Ark ought to be. (Figure 30)

In seeking to uncover the sources of Harrison's work, one must constantly bear in mind the vital fact that his own contribution to the completed design was as great—yes, usually greater—than that of the manuals. Employing familiar forms he worked out an original and soul-satisfying treatment for the interior of the Synagogue. It was a triumph of creative adaptation.

It is a truism that an architect rarely enjoys a free hand when he plans a building. In this case, for example, Hebrew religious custom obtruded itself by requiring conformity with two conditions that must have done great violence to Harrison's academic ideas of symmetry and proportion, both with respect to the building and to its location. Because Griffin Street ran northeasterly he had to place the Synagogue sideways on the lot at an angle of about thirty degrees with the street in order to permit the Ark at the rear of the edifice to face due east as demanded by the ritual. (Figure 27) One compensation did result; the two-story school wing, which he had been forced to annex to the north side of the temple and which virtually destroyed the balance and symmetry of the whole, was largely obscured from view, and the exquisite porch of the Synagogue served further to draw the observer's eye away from the wing.[8]

The addition of the school explains the laying of six cornerstones on August 1, 1759. Two weeks later construction was in full

7. Langley, *Treasury of Designs*, Plate 108; Kent, *Designs of Inigo Jones*, Plate 63; Ware, *Designs of Inigo Jones and others*, Plate 53. For a stimulating and learned discussion of the sources of the Newport Synagogue, consult Fiske Kimball, "Colonial Amateurs and Their Models," 158-60, 185-86.

8. To avoid destroying the beautiful effect of his interior, however, Harrison did not cut a door from the school through to the Synagogue. A niche was placed where the window would normally have been. The women entered the gallery from the second story of the school wing.

swing. The Synagogue was the first of Harrison's New England buildings in which brick was used: by the following August nearly two hundred thousand bricks had been purchased by the committee. Loss of the Congregation's records deprives us of a knowledge of exactly what the architect planned; he may have contemplated covering the brick with stucco to simulate stonework according to a new London fashion that soon became widespread.

Notwithstanding the generosity of Jews on two continents, a shortage of funds delayed construction after 1761. Even though £65.17.0 were allocated for the purchase of rum and sugar for the workmen, one of whom was a Negro slave, Malbo, the Synagogue rose so slowly that in July, 1762, the porch had not yet been added.[9] The painful progress of the building can be traced to its opening in December, 1763, in the account book of Napthali Hart and Company, wherein are entered disbursements totalling £6,256.18.7 in lawful money for materials and for the labor of carpenters, masons, bricklayers, blockmakers, painters, glaziers, and chairmakers. These records never refer to the architect. He asked no fee, and it is clear that following his custom he prepared only the plans, leaving the superintending of the job to the skilled house-carpenter Joseph Hammond, Jr.[10]

When the Synagogue was finally dedicated on December 2, 1763, with the impressive ceremonies described on the first page of this book, Peter Harrison was apparently forgotten. Nowhere in the remaining records does his name appear; the only contemporary reference to his share in the temple is by a British clergyman who visited Newport in 1760.[11] Yet cultivated Newporters who

9. *Literary Diary of Ezra Stiles*, I, 11n., 214; "Notes on Newport Synagogue," *American Hebrew*, 61, p. 101.

10. Napthali Hart & Co., Account Book, Newport Historical Society. Portions of these accounts are published in Friedman, "The Newport Synagogue," 52.

11. Andrew Burnaby, *Travels through the Middle Settlements in North America, in the Years 1759 and 1760* (London, 1775), 68.

took an interest in architecture were not insensitive to the beauty of the edifice; its interior (Figure 30) was so striking that Ezra Stiles described it in detail:

The Synagogue is about perhaps forty feet long and 30 wide, of Brick on a Foundation of free Stone: it was begun about two years ago [1759], and is now finished except the Porch and the Capitals of the Pillars. The front representation of the holy of holies, or its Partition Veil, consists only of wainscotted Breast Work on the East End, in the lower part of which four long Doors cover an upright Square Closet the depth of which is about a foot or the thickness of the Wall, and in this Apartment (vulgarly called the Ark) were deposited three Copies and Rolls of the Pentateuch, written on Vellum or rather tanned Calf Skin; one of these Rolls I was told by Dr. Touro was presented in Amsterdam and is Two Hundred years old; the Letters have the Rabbinical Flourishes.

A Gallery for the Women runs around the whole Inside, except the East End, supported by Columns of the Ionic order, over which are placed correspondent Columns of the Corinthian order supporting the Ceiling of the Roof. The depth of the Corinthian Pedestal is the height of the Balustrade which runs round the Gallery. The Pulpit for Reading the Law, is a raised Pew with an extended front Table; this placed about the center of the Synagogue or nearer the West End, being a Square embalustraded Comporting with the Length of the indented Chancel before and at the foot of the Ark.

On the middle of the North Side and affixed to the Wall is a raised seat for the Paanas or Ruler, and for the Elders; the Breast and Back interlaid with Chinese Mosaic Work. A Wainscotted Seat runs round [the] Sides of the Synagogue below, and another in the Gallery. There are no other Seats or pews. . . . There are to be five lamps pendant from a lofty Ceiling. . . . It is superbly finished withinside at a cost of £2,000 sterling.[12]

In all the colonies there was nothing like this Hebrew house of worship. It was a *tour de force* indeed! Whether the designer of this "Edifice, the most perfect of the Temple kind perhaps in America," was present to enjoy his triumph is extremely doubtful; nor could he, wherever he was, have foreseen that, despite its

12. *Literary Diary of Ezra Stiles*, I, 6*n*., 11*n*.

exterior being "totally spoilt" by the school wing, as Burnaby thought, and even more degraded in the nineteenth century by the removal of its fine cornice and the sad application of cream- and brown-colored paint to its walls and trim, the interior would remain today, as it was in 1759, a thing of surpassing beauty—one of the loveliest church interiors in the United States.

There could be no more fitting symbol of the sweet reasonable- ness pervading the religious atmosphere of eighteenth-century Newport than the spectacle of a congregation professing an oriental faith asking a Christian of the Anglican persuasion to plan its syna- gogue, and of the Episcopalian, entirely without remuneration, responding with the finest interior design of his career—and that based on pagan Greek and Roman forms.

When Peter Harrison was drawing up the plans for the Syna- gogue a meeting of the Society of Freemasons and other prominent Newporters deplored the absence in the Rhode Island capital of any building "sufficiently large and commodious for public enter- tainment, where the Governor and Council, or General Assembly, may occasionally meet and dine; and where any of his Majesty's Governors or other officials may be publicly entertained, as they pass through this government." They concerted to erect a suitable structure, to be called "Mason's Hall," for the purposes enumer- ated and also for the meetings of the Freemasons. On June 11, 1759, they petitioned the General Assembly for permission to conduct a lottery to raise the £2,400 needed to finance the build- ing.[13] Although he was no joiner Harrison signed the petition. Realization that the planning of the hall would devolve upon him no doubt prompted this action. Permission to open the lottery was granted, tickets were sold, and on October 2, 1759, the first draw- ing was announced.[14] Harrison must have worked up the plans

13. Petitions to the General Assembly, X, 82; *R. I. Col. Recs.*, VI, 209-10.
14. *Newport Mercury*, June 26, Oct. 30, 1759.

during the summer, because the foundations had been laid by the time the Reverend Andrew Burnaby viewed them, early in 1760.[15]

No further evidence of this undertaking has come to light. Possibly because funds were not forthcoming the building was never completed. As late as 1765, the members of St. John's Lodge were still dining at a tavern on the anniversary of their patron saint.[16] We can only speculate on the kind of hall the architect's ingenuity would have added to his growing list of civil architecture at Newport. Burnaby, who saw the plans and foundations, pronounced it "a very pretty building."

The town of Newport had by 1760 grown into a small city exhibiting many of the conditions and problems that we call urban. Its seven thousand inhabitants gained their livings largely from activities connected with the sea. The Reverend Mr. Stiles tells us that the four thousand tons of shipping owned in the town required 177,791 "superficial feet" of wharves. Local and foreign vessels continually discharged their cargoes into the 439 warehouses and auxiliary buildings lining the piers and the waterfront. Taken collectively Newport's merchants were prosperous; their trading stock amounted to £3,091,636; investments in factorage totalled £192,668; money out at interest added up to £709,527.[17] The island port had come of age. Yet, as is often the case, public works did not keep pace with the rapid growth of population and with mounting wealth. Two conditions in particular cried for amelioration. Market facilities were outmoded; and no agency existed to insure a plentiful supply of food for the "poorer sort" in times of war or crop failure.

15. "A Number of Carpenter's and Bricklayers are wanted to build Freemason's Hall," read an advertisement in the *Newport Mercury*, July 3, 1759.

16. *Newport Mercury*, Dec. 23, 1765; Burnaby, *Travels*, 67.

17. In satisfying his passion for statistics, Stiles took these figures from the Assessor's valuation of Newport, Aug.-Sept., 1761. *Itineraries*, 14, 22-24.

In seeking a solution of these problems the town fathers had before them the example of the metropolis of New England, which had been forced to deal with like situations several decades earlier. By town action Boston had opened a public granary as early as 1729, and, in 1742, had accepted with noticeable reluctance Peter Faneuil's generous gift of a market house designed by John Smibert.[18] The immense value of these facilities to the Bay Town commended the undertaking of something similar at Rhode Island in 1760.

Private initiative accomplished what civic action failed to do. At a meeting on February 20 of the Proprietors of the Long Wharf, who included many leading merchants, it was voted to present Newport with a piece of land lying adjacent to the south side of the Long Wharf, between Thames Street and the harbor, "for erecting thereon a handsome building, the lower part thereof to be appropriated for a market house and no other use whatsoever, for ever, unless it shall be found convenient to appropriate some part of it for a watch house, and that the upper part of said building shall be made into stores for dry goods, and let out to the best advantage, and all rents, . . . together with all profits . . . shall be lodged in the town Treasury . . . towards a stock for purchasing grain for supplying a public granary." An additional requirement stipulated that the "building be erected agreeable to a plan to be agreed upon by the . . . Proprietors," at a cost of four thousand Spanish dollars or £24,000 old tenor currency.[19]

A committee of the Proprietors applied to the General Assembly for authority to raise by lottery the sum needed to construct "a convenient well situated market house."[20] This the Assembly

18. Boston opened a second granary in 1733. Bridenbaugh, *Cities in the Wilderness*, 353-54.

19. Records of the Proprietors of the Long Wharf, 273, Transcript made for the Proprietor's in March, 1857, Newport, R. I.

20. Petitions to the General Assembly, X, 103; *R. I. Col. Recs.*, VI, 238-39.

granted, and on March 11, 1760, the *Newport Mercury* announced the lottery, which was to be drawn in four classes, and enthusiastically urged its readers to participate freely. "Every Body must be sensible of the absolute Necessity of a well regulated Market in this large Town," James Franklin stated, "It will certainly be attended with numerous and equal Advantages to Persons of all Ranks, and will prevent the many Abuses and Impositions that too frequently happen." Rents should yield an annual income of £1,000, and under careful management the project should benefit all parts of the Colony in time of scarcity. "It will, . . . in the Compass of a few years, afford an ample Supply of Grain, not only for the Poor, but for the whole Town of Newport, which, from its Situation on a Island, (Experience has dearly taught) has been often and much distressed for want of a well supplied Grainary."

On July 10 the Proprietors directed Henry Collins, Captain Joseph Bull, Augustus Johnston and Josias Lyndon "to wait on Capt. Peter Harrison with a plan of the lot . . . and advise with him in respect to erecting thereon a market house." The lot measured thirty-eight feet front along Thames Street and extended in depth fifty feet westerly. The committee reported back to a meeting at the Black Horse Tavern on July 24 "that a gentleman well skilled in architecture has been consulted, who has given his opinion that the dimensions of the lot . . . will by no means answer the end intended, but for a regular building according to the rules of architecture, the lot should be thirty-three feet on the north [front] and sixty-six feet deep." [21] For the first time in his career Peter Harrison had been given an opportunity to pass on the site for a building. He was determined not only that Newport should have a fine market house, but that it should be attractively situated on a location in keeping with its importance. After some discussion

21. Proprietors of the Long Wharf, 81-82.

the Proprietors unanimously voted to grant to the town immediately a lot of the size specified by Mr. Harrison, and on September 10 they made a supplementary gift of two small gores of land "that the building may stand more commodiously than other wise it could have done." [22]

Planning a market house "according to the rules of architecture" presented Harrison with no challenge comparable to the preparation of designs for King's Chapel, St. Michael's or the Synagogue. Just as today certain structures designated for specific functions, such as a bank, a hospital, or the more lowly gasoline service station, conjure up a mental stereotype, so in the eighteenth century did the idea of a market house or town hall. Everybody knew what one ought to look like. Old England was dotted with market houses conforming to an accepted pattern, based on function, of two stories resting on an arcaded ground floor; such, too, was the style of John Smibert's Faneuil Hall and of the famous town house at Philadelphia. Peter Harrison knew full well what his fellow-townsmen would want and expect. He conceived his design accordingly. English town halls such as those of Abingdon in Berkshire, Andrew Jelfe's excellent building at Rye in Sussex, and especially that at South Moulton in Devon furnished the initial inspiration. He had certainly seen many of these and similar buildings in his travels, and, possibly even, Sir Christopher Wren's town hall at Windsor, which strongly resembles the Brick Market of Newport. [23]

Once more the architect received measurable aid from his books in filling out the details of his conception. Particularly suggestive was an engraving of old Somerset House in his *Vitruvius*

22. *Ibid.*, 82, 95.

23. Photographs of some of these English town halls are to be found in W. R. Ware, *The Georgian Period* (Boston, 1899-1902), II, pt. VIII, Plates 19, 21; see also, *Sir Christopher Wren*, published for the Royal British Institute of Architects (London, 1923), 20.

Britannicus. Here Inigo Jones and John Webb had adapted a design, never employed by Palladio, which they used both at Covent Garden and Lindsay House. (Figure 37) Peter Harrison undoubtedly saw William Kent's application of many of the details on a smaller scale to Lady Isabella Finch's town house at No. 44 Berkeley Square when he was in London. He indulged in no slavish copying, however, for his market plan shows many departures from Colin Campbell's engraving in *Vitruvius Britannicus*. He discarded the rusticated arches entirely. Details for the windows he probably took from Gibbs's *Rules for Drawing*, while other plates in the same folio may have served as models for the Ionic pilasters he substituted for the Corinthian order employed at Somerset House.[24]

The finished plan was elegant in the eighteenth-century sense. (Figure 36) Although the market is academic in treatment, it actually represents Peter Harrison's creative adaptation of Palladian elements and detail to the prevailing market-town hall pattern.[25] He arrived at a pleasing effect by the use of entasis on the pilasters and by combining the pilasters at the corners of the structure to simulate a column. In fact the use of pilasters to relieve the monotony of the walls was not only successful but it was a novelty in the colonies. The treatment of the arcaded ground floor subtly produces the illusion of a heavy base by underemphasizing the arches and recesses. Since brick was to be his material he wisely decided against rustic work and produced a very satisfactory result merely by carrying a belt course around the base. Unusually happy was the substitution of Ionic for Corinthian pilasters. As finally

24. Colin Campbell, *Vitruvius Britannicus* (folio, London, 1715-25), Plate 15; Gibbs, *Rules for Drawing*, Plates 2, 10, 12, 14, 40, 42, 45. Pilasters are also used at Lindsay House. See Summerson, *Georgian London*, Plates 1, 2, 7, for Covent Garden, Lindsay House, and Finch House.
25. In his able discussion Fiske Kimball places more emphasis on Harrison's bookish sources than I have. "Colonial Amateurs and Their Models," 154, 158-60.

completed the Brick Market was genuinely impressive and definitely bore the stamp of Harrison's own architectural thought.

Shortly after the drawings for the Brick Market were finished the Reverend Andrew Burnaby visited Newport and recorded his impressions of the town. As a cultured English gentleman of taste he naturally commented on its architecture:

> There are a few buildings in it worth notice. The court-house is indeed handsome, and of brick; and there is a public library, built in the form of a Grecian temple by no means inelegant. It is of the Doric order, and has a portico in front with four pillars, supporting a pediment; but the whole is spoilt by two small wings, which are annexed to it.[26] The foundation of a very pretty building is laid for the use of the free-masons, to serve also occasionally for an assembly-room; and there is to be erected a market house upon a very elegant design. The places of public worship, except the Jews synagogue, are all of wood; and not one of them is worth looking at. They consist chiefly of a church, two presbyterian meeting-houses, one quakers ditto, three anabaptist ditto, one Moravian ditto, and the synagogue above-mentioned. This building was designed, as indeed were several of the others, by a Mr. Harrison, an ingenious English gentleman who lives here. It will be extremely elegant within when compleated: but the outside is totally spoilt by a school, which the Jews insisted on having annexed to it for the education of their children. Upon a small island, before the town, is part of a fine fortification, designed to consist of a pentagon-fort, and an upper and lower battery. Only two of the curtains, and a ravelin, are yet finished; and it is doubtful whether the whole will ever be. At the entrance of the harbour is likewise an exceeding good lighthouse. These are the chief public buildings.[27]

Had the future Archdeacon of Leicester given this subject a little more thought, he might have considered it remarkable that a seaport of only seven thousand inhabitants was able to muster a display of civic buildings of such architectural distinction. Few,

26. Apparently Burnaby was not aware of the widespread use of such wings in England.
27. Burnaby, *Travels*, 67-68.

FIGURE 12. Christ Church, Cambridge, designed by Peter Harrison in 1759-60, taken from an early view in the *Massachusetts Magazine* for July, 1792.

FIGURES 13-14. A mid-nineteenth-century view and plan of Governor John Wentworth's mansion at Wolfeborough, New Hampshire. Although much of the plan can be credited to Peter Harrison, it is impossible to determine his precise share in the designing of the structure. *From Benjamin F. Parker, History of Wolfeborough*

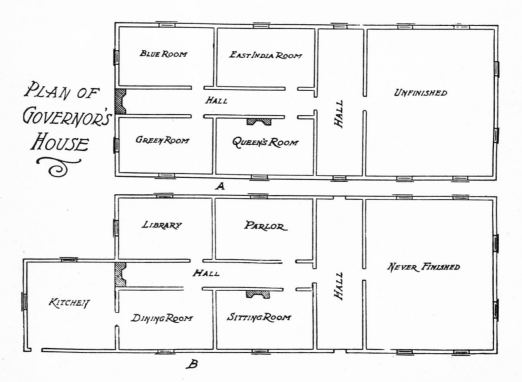

if any, communities of the same size in his native islands could have produced its equal, and, moreover, the public architecture of no city in either Britain or the colonies was so completely the expression of the talents of one man.

Accustomed as he was to interminable delays in the completion of the buildings he designed, Peter Harrison must often have feared that his Brick Market would never be finished. Finances proved the chief obstacle. Although the Assembly authorized a lottery to produce the needed £24,000, by the end of the fifth drawing only £18,000 had been raised. Work on the foundations began in September, 1762; in the following July the building proper commenced and was carried to such a stage that it could not be abandoned without great loss. At this moment the Assembly unfortunately permitted a lottery for the paving of Thames Street, which greatly impeded the sale of tickets for the Market House lottery. Late in 1763 the committee roofed the structure at its own expense, hoping to be reimbursed by the town. None of the upper chambers was finished in August, 1764, when the building committee sought assistance from the Town Meeting.

The delay continued. Two years later no floor had been laid in the Market. "A Friend to the Town" in 1770 inaugurated the usual public works inquiry through the *Newport Mercury*, demanding an explanation of why so much money had been spent and so little accomplished. Petitions, audits, delays innumerable, and, above all, the unwillingness of the Town Meeting to assume its proper obligations forestalled completion of the building. The town did order the "Cornish," windows, doors, and other exterior details finished at the public charge "according to the plan" in September, 1771. Finally, by late July, 1772, the rooms or stores were ready to be rented, and in December the market was at last opened to the public. Harrison and his family had removed to New Haven in 1766 and it is extremely doubtful if the architect ever returned to Newport during the last three years of his life to view his final contribution to American architecture.[28]

In the spring of 1759, while Peter Harrison was preparing the plans for the Jewish Synagogue and the Freemason's Hall at Newport, a group of wealthy and exceedingly prominent and genteel Anglicans dwelling at Cambridge in Massachusetts pledged themselves to subscribe £3,436.8.9 to build a church in the college town. At a meeting in Boston, September 28, 1759, the subscribers appointed a building committee consisting of the Reverend East Apthorp, Colonel Henry Vassall, Major John Vassall, Judge Joseph Lee, Lieutenant-Governor Thomas Oliver, and David Phips, and empowered them to proceed with the undertaking. At the same time it was agreed "that the extreme dimensions of the Church, including the thickness of the Walls, but exclusive of the Chancel and Tower, be Sixty Feet in Length, and Forty-five Feet in Breadth." Being gentlemen of taste and judgment they wisely agreed in addition, "that the Architect be at Liberty to make any alterations in the ... dimensions, ... provided he does not enlarge the area of the Church." Inasmuch as they felt they could not spend more than £500 sterling they further stipulated that "the Building be of wood, and covered on the outside with Rough-cast; that there be only one tier of Windows; and no Galleries, except an organ Loft." [29]

It is clear that in reaching their decision the members of the committee had King's Chapel, where most of them worshipped, very much in mind, and, since several of them knew Peter Harrison

28. There is absolutely no basis for the statement, usually made in Newport, that the Brick Market was "finished" in 1762. *Newport Mercury*, Nov. 2, 1762; Feb. 26, 1770; May 4, July 6, 1772; Newport Town Meeting Records, 786, 862, 962, 1002, 1004; *R. I. Col. Recs.*, VI, 255; VII, 19.

29. Records of Christ Church, Cambridge, I, 7, 25-26, Massachusetts Historical Society.

intimately and regarded him as one of the few in New England who understood what "modern" taste demanded, it was natural that they should have directed "that a Letter be wrote to Mr. Harrison of Newport, requesting a Plan and Elevation of the Outside and Inside, and of the Pulpit and Vestry, of the Church; and that, if Mr. Harrison approves of it, there be no steeple, only a Tower with a Belfry; and that he be informed of the dimensions of a Picture designed for the Chancel (now at Mr. Merritt's at Providence) when the Committee are informed of its size.[30] Perhaps they feared additional expense beyond their means should Peter Harrison design a spire as elaborate as that he had planned for King's Chapel.

Any ordinary man would at this time have claimed a respite from the drafting-board and an opportunity to adjust his affairs. But Peter Harrison was no average man. He wanted to serve his church and friends; nor was the manner of doing so unpleasing to him for his instinct of workmanship was strong. So in spite of the fact that he had recently been drawn for jury duty he accepted the new commission and went to work on the plans.[31]

Meanwhile Colonel Henry Vassall purchased "60 m. merchantable boards, 20 m. clear boards, 1 m. clear Planks, 45 m. inch shingles, and 60 m. of Laths for the inside work," some lime, and also cast about for stone for the foundations—a material difficult to obtain in Massachusetts. At the same time the Reverend Mr. Apthorp bespoke the aid of Harrison's London friend, Barlow Trecothick, in procuring subscriptions toward an organ. The committee sent four letters of instructions to the Newport architect between October and December, receiving five in reply. Mr. Apthorp informed the Society of the Propagation of the Gospel in Foreign Parts on November 24 that the utmost they hoped to

30. Records of Christ Church, Cambridge, I, 25-26.
31. Newport Town Council Records, II, 173.

accomplish so late in the season was the collecting and preparation of the building materials, but, he added enthusiastically, "we have applied to a masterly Architect for a plan, and propose to build a handsome Church." [32]

It was no easy task for Colonel Vassall to procure building materials. Since New England had no known stone satisfactory for construction work, the necessary "large Stones" were acquired by the extraordinary expedient of purchasing the ballast of a vessel recently entered at Boston from Quebec and lightering it at considerable expense up the Charles to Cambridge. Of course, other ballast had to be found for the Quebec ship and her sailors had to be paid for their labor. In fact, virtually all of the supplies arrived by water: lime, the boards bought of Nathaniel Sparhawk in Boston, "5 Casks Nails" costing £58.11.5¾, "Rope to bind 290 Sparrs" for the scaffolding, and bricks from Mr. Wyeth. [33]

During the fall and winter of 1759-1760, while he was putting the finishing touches on the plans, Harrison kept in touch with the building committee by mail. [34] He was now able to work along leisurely and to produce what was to be the freest of his designs. To this end the specifications of the Cambridge gentlemen also contributed. A careful search of his books yields no overall design that might have served him for a general model as did one of Gibbs's for the exterior form of King's Chapel. From the *Rules for Drawing* may have come the models for the Ionic columns used in the interior, line for line without a change, as well as suggestions for the beautiful organ loft. (Figures 40-41) Various other features reflect the influence of Gibbs, such as the tall arches with imposts and archivolts, the cruciform belfry stage, and the heavy

32. Records of Christ Church, I, 26, 30-31, 70.
33. *Ibid.*, 70.
34. In January the Committee wrote to Harrison once, in February twice, and twice again in March. *Ibid.*

Doric cornice. [35] (Figure 39) Peter Harrison's individuality as an architect stands out more prominently in Christ Church than in any of his other works. Here he demonstrated conclusively his power to combine elements and details taken from the folios into a plan for an edifice of noble proportions possessing a vitality of its own. (Figure 38)

After Mr. Ralph Inman paid Peter Mumford, the post-rider, 13s.6d. in March, 1760, "for Bringing up the Plan," the gentlemen of the building committee learned that they were truly to have a handsome church. As he had done earlier for King's Chapel, Peter Harrison sent a complete set of drawings: elevations and plans, both exterior and interior, and detailed designs for the pulpit, vestry, and organ loft besides. [36] Though prepared by a gentleman and an amateur who asked no remuneration these embodied excellent draftsmanship, careful detail, and professional completeness. Such pleasing work from a generous friend should not pass unrewarded, the committee opined, and in the accounts for May, 1761, their gratitude is recorded: "To Peter Harrison drawing the Plan £45." [37]

Perhaps it was the generous portions of rum from Stedman's tavern with which the workmen were plied that speeded the work on the church. In any event, on August 30 the Reverend Mr. Apthorp reported to the Venerable Society that "the foundation and frame of the building are now completed and as we apprehend no delays of any kind, the whole work is in such forwardness that we make no doubt of accomplishing our first design of having the Church fit for divine Service before the Winter. As near as I

35. James Gibbs, *Rules for Drawing*, Plates 16, 17, 36; Kimball, "Colonial Amateurs and Their Models," 158, 185, 188.

36. There are some useful measured drawings of details of Christ Church in R. C. Kingman, *New England Georgian Architecture* (New York, 1913), Plates 20-27.

37. Records of Christ Church, I, 70-71.

can judge, if we do not wait for the Glass for the Windows, which is soon expected from England, it will be opened in the month of November. Particular care has been taken to make the Structure useful and durable, as well as decently elegant; and in case of future accessions to the Congregation, it may be easily enlarged." [38]

Unapprehended delays, as usual, occurred when the crate of glass and ten thousand twenty-penny nails "long since expected from England" failed to arrive until January, 1761. "Rafting 18 Pillars to Cambridge," alone, cost £56.5.1; then, Mr. Inman had to pay Edward Manning £16.16 for turning and Skippic Townsend and one Brewer £6 and £1.12 for boring them—operations both difficult and unusual to perform in the little village. By August James Sherman was at work on the painting and Louis Robichaud, Acadian exile, who in later years taught French to the artist Trumbull, put in thirteen days digging the cellar at a charge of £16. [39]

The edifice was finished, "as far as necessary," by October and when Anglicans assembled from near and far on the fifteenth to listen to the Reverend Mr. Apthorp's dedication sermon, all agreed with him that Peter Harrison's "temple" possessed "a beauty and elegance not unbecoming the majesty of religion." [40] Although the committee had been instructed not to exceed £500 sterling, the building actually cost the gentlemen of Cambridge nearer £1,300. In this unanticipated cost lies the explanation of the failure of the workmen to "Rough-cast" the exterior and to carve the pillars

38. William S. Perry, ed., *Historical Collections Relating to the American Colonial Church* (Hartford, 1870-78), III, 457, 463.

39. Records of Christ Church, I, 74, 76.

40. There being no bishop present, the service could not be a true consecration. East Apthorp to Dr. Bearcroft, S. P. G. MSS, B 23, f. 26, Library of Congress Transcripts; East Apthorp, *The Constitution of a Christian Church Illustrated in a Sermon at the Opening of Christ Church, Cambridge on Thursday, 15 October MDCCLXI* (Boston, 1761). For further details about Christ Church, see Samuel F. Batchelder, *Christ Church, Cambridge* (Cambridge, 1893); and *Bits of Cambridge History* (Cambridge, 1930); as well as Nicholas Hoppin, *A Sermon on the Re-Opening of Christ Church, Cambridge, Mass.* (Boston, 1858).

and capitals. Even though the committee desired to omit a spire, it seems that Peter nevertheless provided one, because his friend, the Reverend Ezra Stiles includes a steeple in a crude drawing of the church that he made in 1761.[41]

Very wisely the building committee had allowed their "masterly architect" wide latitude in his plans for Christ Church. He planned so soundly and so substantially in his customary Burlington manner that contemporaries declared "it was one of the best constructed churches in New England." Built largely of sturdy oak it has resisted time well, and, as planned, was successfully enlarged in the nineteenth century. Harrison suited the exterior form to the ecclesiastical needs of a small country town, just as he designed King's Chapel for the more sophisticated taste of New England's metropolis. The interior of Christ Church with its stately rows of Ionic pillars surmounted with quaint fragments of entablature, and the deep semicircular chancel, lighted by one of his favorite Venetian windows, was and is truly striking and impressive.[42] (Figure 40) Even the exterior, minus the spire, was imposing enough to warrant an engraving in the *Massachusetts Magazine* for July, 1792. (Figure 12)

It has been said that Peter Harrison was the "prince" of the colonial amateur architects. Through early training in cognate crafts, supplemented by his associations, wide travel, and thorough study of the literature of the Palladian school headed by the Earl of Burlington, he acquired that technical competence and facility which lends to his works many of the qualities of the professional. As far as training was concerned he was a professional. Nowhere is this more evident than in his careful attention to accuracy, pro-

41. Stiles's plan is reasonably correct, as are most of the features of the side elevation, but he depicts a much plainer spire than one would expect Harrison to design. Batchelder, *Christ Church*, 19; Stiles, *Itineraries*, 102.

42. Batchelder, *Christ Church*, 13, 14.

portion, and correctness of detail. For suggestions and occasional inspirations he turned to those admirable engraved folios that formed the corpus of Palladianism. From them he selected ideas or models which suited his particular purpose, but in so doing he was neither a direct borrower nor a mere imitator.

The majority of the designs that achieved a place in the sumptuous works of Lord Burlington, Leoni, Campbell, and Gibbs did so because they mirrored the manner of the moment as well as because they included unique features worked out by the compilers. Many of them, perhaps most in a work like Campbell's *Vitruvius Britannicus*, had been published as an important record of architecture and as a mark of distinction deserving of inclusion in such splendid volumes. The great folios were never intended to instruct in building methods and planning; these lesser objectives were left to the many handbooks prepared by such practical architect-builders as Isaac Ware, Batty Langley, and William Halfpenny, which aimed to provide examples for the builder to copy. This distinction Peter Harrison thoroughly understood. We can trace in the great folios his sources of inspiration, his prototypes or models, but only in the case of details, as in the altars of King's Chapel and Christ Church and the Ark at the Synagogue, does he appear to have borrowed freely from a manual like Batty Langley's. Like the members of the Burlington school he created architectural solutions. In every sense of the term Peter Harrison qualified as an architect.

The architectural activities of Harrison in his adopted town of Newport interestingly parallel those of Andrea Palladio at Vicenza. Both men were more or less concerned with the same kind of building. Each was circumscribed by insufficient means and was thereby forced to work largely with inferior materials. In the Rhode Islander's case this meant either wood as a substitute for brick or brick in the place of dressed stone: the Redwood Library and Christ

Church clearly show that he intelligently designed them for the medium he was forced to employ; the same holds true for his use of brick in the Synagogue and Market House. Yet, though he readily adjusted his design to the limitations of the medium, he never sacrificed correctness and proportion: witness his pure Scamozzi capitals for the Venetian window of the Redwood Library and for the interior colonnades of Christ Church, the exquisite Synagogue porch, and the pilasters of the Brick Market.

As a gentleman who obliged his contemporaries with designs for the buildings they wished to erect, Harrison was in a position to be uncompromising, rigid, and dogmatic in his adherence to classical rules, but, as we have seen, though it must have pained him to sacrifice the proportions and balance of his plan for the Synagogue, he bowed to the wishes of the Congregation and attached the school to the edifice.

The architectural achievement of Peter Harrison represented but one aspect of the career of a man who sought in America to live like an English country gentleman. "No one can properly be styled a gentleman," wrote a London critic in 1734, "who has not made use of every opportunity to enrich his own capacity and settle the elements of Taste, which he may improve at his leisure." [43] A knowledge of architecture being thus, like the *chapeau bras,* a symbol of gentility, Peter Harrison built upon his early training and assembled at his estate the largest and finest architectural library in English America. [44] James Ralph might have added to his observation just quoted that the aristocratic, landed ideal inculcated not only the right to privilege but also the responsibility of service. When colony, community, or church called, Peter

43. James Ralph, *A Critical Review of the Public Buildings, Statues, and Ornaments in and about London* (London, 1734), quoted in B. Sprague Allen, *Tides of English Taste,* I, 57.
44. Appendix C.

Harrison gladly responded with his best effort. Remuneration or public acclaim he neither asked nor expected—and rarely received. It mattered not. For him there was infinite satisfaction in devoting his very real talents to the public weal during his hard-earned leisure.

V

The Price of Loyalty

IT WOULD BE difficult to overestimate the speculative nature of commercial risks in the late colonial period. Business offered no guarantee of stability. Amid the vicissitudes of wind, wave, war, and the portended restrictions on trade, it was hard to win a fortune. Insurance was in its infancy, and no merchant could plan his enterprises with certainty. Profits were often large, to be sure; so also were losses. In the gambling phrase each venture meant taking the long shot. Far more attractive was service under the Crown at a stated salary, payable in sterling, plus the pleasing prospect of lucrative fees—this meant real comfort and security. In addition, office-holding offered far more than a salary and perquisites. To attain a place in the King's employ in the eighteenth century was for most people a definite step upward. In the American colonies the chosen places in society went almost without exception to the royal officials.

Some such reasoning lay behind Joseph Harrison's journey to England in 1755. In the search for preferment he assiduously cultivated the acquaintance of gentlemen in high places and made the fullest use of his wife's connections at Wyeston. By adroitly reminding the Duke of Newcastle of election services hitherto unrewarded, Jonathan Acklam succeeded in procuring an appointment to the collectorship of the port of New Haven, Connecticut, for the husband of his favorite niece.[1] An improved status, £50 sterling a year, and a steady income from fees appealed greatly to Joseph Harrison, who had not married on to a landed estate. He contemplated the possibility that by constant application and faithfulness at his post, and with influential patrons to back him, he could advance rapidly to power and affluence in the colonial establishment. In time he would acquire broad acres of his own. And who could tell, possibly some day he might even become a royal governor!

When he took the oath of office at New Haven on April 20, 1760, the future looked bright indeed. But this fateful act of Joseph's irrevocably changed the course of the whole Harrison family. Henceforth they were the King's men, and as "Loyalists" or "Tories" their destiny was not to be social eminence and financial security but rather ignominy and disaster—which would end in tragedy.

Management of the affairs of the partnership continued to devolve wholly upon Peter after Joseph's return from England with his deputation as collector for New Haven. In truth, times were so bad at Newport after the passage of the Sugar Act in 1764 and the strengthening of the customs service that there was scarcely enough activity at the Thames Street counting house to keep one of the brothers busy.[2] Like his Charles Town acquaintance Benjamin d'Harriette, Peter Harrison, "knowing when he had enough," also gradually withdrew from trade, and his transition to the status of a landed gentleman became complete. By this time his farm had reached the stage where its cash crops yielded about £172

1. Jonathan Acklam to Duke of Newcastle, Aug. 27, 1757, British Museum, Additional Manuscripts, 32873, f. 332, Library of Congress Transcripts.
2. See the remarkable analysis of Rhode Island's economic plight set forth in the "Remonstrance" the colony sent to the Board of Trade in 1764, protesting against the Sugar Act. *R. I. Col. Recs.*, VI, 378-83.

sterling annually.[3] Further income, of course, he derived from the rents of houses in town.

Throughout the years 1761-1765 Peter Harrison contented himself with family and agricultural pursuits. Long a reader of plays, he must have been among the gentlemen who patronized David Douglass' company of comedians when they performed *The Provok'd Wife* at Newport in September, 1761, in a temporary theater on Easton's Point. This, New England's first public play, ended with a tragic after-piece when Peter's friend John Whipple fell off the Point Bridge and was drowned while he was making his way home in the darkness.[4] In January, 1762, Harrison was one of the forty-six gentlemen who pledged themselves to enlarge Trinity Church "to the eastward, . . . for which they are to have the pews." Anyone of his scientific bent would naturally have attended the "Course of Experiments in that instructive and entertaining Branch of Natural Philosophy, called Electricity, . . . accompanied with Lectures on the Nature and Properties of Electric Fire, By William Johnson," held at the Colony House in February, 1764.[5]

A serious illness doubtless speeded his retirement. Although Dr. William Hunter did not record the nature of the malady, his Account Book shows that between September 6 and December 15, 1765, he made thirty-four visits to the farm, two of them at

3. With all his canniness in matters mercantile, John Banister had withdrawn from trade late in the fifties to live at his Middletown estate. When he died "at his Seat" in 1767, his will revealed the landed ideal. He advised his son Thomas "not to enter into a Trade," since he was leaving him an ample fortune. Hermione Pelham Banister died July 8, 1765. *Newport Mercury*, July 15, 1765; Nov. 16, 1767; *N. E. Hist. & Gen. Register*, 69 (1905), 345-51; *South-Carolina Gazette*, Feb. 9, 1756.

4. *Newport Mercury*, Aug. 11, Nov. 3, 1761; Edward Peterson, *History of Rhode Island* (New York, 1853), 103.

5. Mason, *Annals of Trinity Church*, 124; *Newport Mercury*, Feb. 6, 13, 20, 1764.

night, and that his usual prescription was "a Mixture of Camphr." With the camphor and so many calls from Newport's most eminent practitioner Peter ran up a large bill, which by April, 1766, amounted to £21.2.10½. During April and May Dr. Hunter's visits began again: on May 15 he was summoned twice. Eleven calls plus three more for the Negro house servants, Apollo and Lucy, brought the medical charges up to £30.15.4¼. Although Peter recovered from this sickness he was thereafter frequently in poor health.[6]

Any colonial family of means always acquired a few works on "household physick" like "Hill's Family Herbal" and "Buchan's Domestic Medicine," or "Tissot on Health," but it must have been Peter's valetudinarianism that made him purchase, in addition to such old reliables, the newest medical works, especially a "Treatise on Teeth" and "Tissot on Literary and Sedentary persons."[7]

In addition to poor health and the declining state of trade, Peter Harrison's associates at Newport and elsewhere in New England proved most influential not only in diverting his attention from the counting house but in turning the remainder of his life into an entirely new channel. It will be recalled that among his oldest friends were John Maudsley, Dr. Thomas Moffatt, Attorney-General Augustus Johnston, Dr. William Hunter, and Martin Howard, the leading lawyer of Rhode Island. They were joined by George Rome who in 1761 unpropitiously came over as the agent of several London merchants to collect long-standing debts owing them in Newport.[8] Through Joseph's new alliances Peter was soon on intimate terms with the King's customs and admiralty-court officers at Newport and privy to their increasing difficulties

6. Dr. William Hunter, Medical Account Book, 1764-68, p. 68, Newport Historical Society.

7. "Lind on Hot Climates" and "Lind on Scurvy" were doubtless relics of his sea-faring days. See Appendix B.

8. R. I. Land Records, VII, 465-66.

with the local merchants whom Martin Howard branded a "parcel of infamous smugglers." [9]

This little Newport coterie were all Anglicans, all office-holders under the Crown or aspiring to become such, all non-mercantile in occupation except Rome, all "loyal" to Great Britain, all avid in their quest for place and influence. Perhaps their most cohesive bond was that for the most part they were not natives of Newport or even of Rhode Island. Several were Jacobites, and Ezra Stiles was shortly to observe: "Near half are Europeans." [10] These men corresponded regularly with their confreres in the royal service at Portsmouth, Boston, New Haven, and occasionally at New York, exchanging confidential information, and gradually with the changing times coalesced into a solid phalanx which formed the nucleus of the Tory Party in America.

Under the leadership of the gifted aristocrat Martin Howard a junto of fifteen or twenty of these gentlemen, avowedly anti-republican and anti-democratic, conspired to effect a reactionary coup d'état in the colony of Rhode Island by having it made a royal province. Although he lived at New Haven, Joseph Harrison was deep in their councils. When he sailed for London in October, 1764, to consult with his influential friends about obtaining a more important and lucrative post in the customs service, he bore with him a "Petition to the King," drawn up by Howard and Dr. Moffatt, praying for an end of the Rhode Island "Burlesque on Order and Government" and the institution of something better, which he was authorized to submit should the opportunity for a favorable reception arise. [11]

9. Martin Howard, *A Letter from a Gentleman in Halifax to his Friend in Rhode Island* (Newport, 1765), 17; James Otis, *A Vindication of the British Colonies*, University of Missouri, *Studies*, IV, 145.

10. Ezra Stiles, The Stamp Act, in Stiles Papers, Yale University Library. Quoted by permission.

11. Joseph Harrison's salary was three years in arrears, and he also was having difficulty over fees collected by his deputy at Stamford. Martin Howard to Ben-

When the Stamp Act riots broke out at Newport the following August, the anti-charter "Gentlemen Episcopalians" were the victims of the mob's rage, Howard and Moffatt suffering more severely even than Stamp-Collector Johnston. There can be no question of Peter Harrison's agreement with the ideas of the cabal or of his concurrence in its plans. But his was a passive role. It is of the utmost significance that although the Reverend Ezra Stiles listed Peter as one of those who "wrote home" about the rioting, he did not consider him inimical to the cause of liberty. The architect was a mild and good citizen, holding "the wrong views" of course, but he kept his counsel and did not participate actively in this abortive movement against the charter.[12] Moreover, he had generously performed many notable services to town and colony. Throughout a residence of over a quarter century at Newport Peter Harrison had succeeded in gaining the respect, and in many cases the affection, of the community, which in the eyes of the patriot leaders measurably helped to mitigate the odium of his loyalism, his Anglicanism, his aristocratic view of life, and his ill-advised associations.

Nevertheless, life at Harrison Farm never again proved as attractive as before the terrifying August days of 1765. Peter's friends, Moffatt and Howard, soon crossed to London to seek indemnification for their losses, and the shots fired at their ship as it stood past the battery Peter had built on Goat Island fairly expressed the mood of the town. Should anything promising turn up, Peter

---

jamin Franklin, Nov. 16, 1764, Franklin Papers, I, 108; II, 127, American Philosophical Society.

12. "In Newport," wrote Stiles, "was the greatest Body of Advocates for the Stamp Act of any Town in America. The Customs house Officers, officers of three Men o'War, and about one hundred Gentlemen Episcopalians openly called the opposition Rebellion, &c." He drew up a list of such people, indicating by arrows "the Degrees of Vigour and Activity" of each. Peter Harrison came off easier than his associates. Ezra Stiles, The Stamp Act, Stiles Papers.

would not find it difficult as in former years to leave his beloved acres for a more friendly community.

In England Joseph Harrison found a way out for his brother. His mission had been overwhelmingly successful, as he saw it, culminating with membership in the official family of the Marquis of Rockingham, where his vast knowledge of American conditions had been influential in bringing about the repeal of the Stamp Act.[13] In April, 1766, Joseph wrote to John Temple, Surveyor General of the Customs at Boston, that "Lord Rockingham has indulged me with a permission to resign my office at New Haven to my brother." He then went on to describe Peter's fitness for the post:

On this occasion I must beg leave to recommend my brother to your favour and notice, being perfectly well assured that you will find him not only a very honest but a very accomplished officer, and one that will keep up the dignity of his station, and has tallents and abilities that will render him very important and popular in that country, particularly his knowledge in agriculture, ship-building and architecture, with a general acquaintance on all affairs of trade and commerce.[14]

The New Haven vacancy was created when the Marquis of Rockingham, true to his promise, procured the appointment of Joseph Harrison as collector of the port of Boston—possibly the most lucrative, certainly the most important collectorship in America. He landed with his family on October 28, and the next day John Rowe, leading social reporter of the Bay Town noted in his diary: "After dinner I went and pd. a visit to Mr. Harrison

13. Joseph Harrison was at this time on intimate terms with Mr. Dowdeswell, Chancellor of the Exchequer; Sir Grey Cooper, Secretary to the Treasury Board; Sir George Saville; Edmund Burke; and most of the London merchants trading to America. *Bowdoin and Temple Papers*, I, 42, 70, 72; Phineas Lyman to Thomas Fitch, Feb. 26, 1766, Fitch Papers, XI, 77a, b, d, Connecticut State Library.

14. Commissioners of Customs to Governor of Connecticut, April 12, 1766, Trumbull Papers, II, 86, Conn. State Library; *Bowdoin and Temple Papers*, I, 73.

Our new Collector." [15] Now that both brothers were securely established in the royal service everything seemed to augur well for the future of the Harrisons.

The New Haven Customs District, which ran along Long Island Sound from Killingworth to Greenwich, had been under the supervision of Comptroller George Mills during Joseph Harrison's long absence. Mills had closed the office on Long Wharf during the Stamp Act crisis, but in February, 1766, the newspaper reported that "Business has been transacted as formerly at the Customs House, for a Month past." No popular acclaim had greeted this resumption of revenue collecting; instead the last Wednesday in January a number of persons collected in the evening "and forcibly took a Seafaring Man from a Tavern, who was convicted as a mercenary informer" by them, then whipped and expelled him from town, despite the protests of the constable. Heading this mob was Benedict Arnold, a West-India merchant and former employer of the victim. Arnold and Mills indulged in an exchange of opinions in the *Connecticut Gazette* which culminated in a declaration by the Comptroller that although "there is a beneficial illicit trade carried on, contrary to what we imagined to be done, in any considerable degree," nevertheless every master of a vessel will be required on entering the harbor to subscribe under oath to the truth of his manifest and a tide-waiter will board every ship to check the cargo against the manifest.[16] Such was the situation at the Customs House when, after some delay caused by

15. Sir Grey Cooper and Sir George Saville also helped with the appointment. The warrant was signed at London, July 11, 1766. Crown Commissions, 1667-1774, p. 68, Massachusetts Archives, Boston. See also, Annie R. Cunningham, ed., *Letters and Diary of John Rowe* (Boston, 1903), 114.

16. Arnold owned the forty-five ton sloop *Charming Sally*, Captain Samuel Toles, which traded to St. Croix. *Connecticut Courant*, Feb. 10, 1766; *Connecticut Gazette*, Feb. 2, 21, 1766; District of New Haven, Foreigners Inward, Nov. 25, 1765, National Archives.

illness and the settlement of business affairs, Peter Harrison moved his family to New Haven, where he qualified for his post on October 10, 1766.[17]

New Haven was a prosperous and growing town. Its rapid expansion in recent years to about seven thousand inhabitants resulted largely from the increasing importance of an excellent harbor. At the Customs House on the Long Wharf, vessels regularly cleared with cargoes of cattle, hogs, cheese, and lumber for the British and "foreign" West Indies, and, on occasion, with lumber and rum to exchange at the Barbary States for mules, which were sold in the West Indies for much-needed bills of exchange. Commerce and ancillary industries, particularly shipbuilding, provided employment for hundreds of seamen and artisans—the stuff, incidentally, of which colonial mobs were made. Long a country village, even though laid-out "Regularly" with wide streets like Philadelphia, New Haven was "built only here and there" around a beautiful Green and still presented "a very indifferent aspect." Its four churches were undistinguished and there were no civic buildings of note. The community took great pride in being the seat of Yale College, that fortress of conservative Congregationalism that had given the colony so many able Episcopalian ministers. As Peter Harrison studied the progress of the town and the several interests of the conservative little oligarchy of gentlemen who presided over its destinies, through the columns of John and Thomas Green's *Connecticut Journal and New Haven Post-Boy*, he could

17. To qualify as a collector of the customs the appointee had to go through the following procedure: 1) secure a Treasury Warrant to the Board of Customs Commissioners for his appointment; 2) procure a Deputation from the Board; 3) pay fees for the Warrant and Deputation (which, in Peter's case, Joseph undoubtedly did); 4) give bond with two securities for £500; 5) register the Deputation with the governor and take the oath of office. A certificate signed by Governor Jabez Fitch indicated completion of the last step and entitled Peter Harrison to draw his salary. Information generously supplied by Professor Dora Mae Clark of Wilson College. See also, A. O., Declared Accounts, Bundle 76, Roll 1076; Trumbull Papers, II, 86.

conclude that although it lacked the culture and urbanity of Newport it was nevertheless a pleasant place in which to live.[18]

New Haven shipping, which had been increasing during Joseph
Harrison's collectorship, now slipped into a decline that continued
down to the outbreak of the War of Independence. Ships entering
inwards in 1766 numbered only twenty-five as compared with
fifty-two the previous year.[19] Collections in 1763 had amounted
to £343.1.0. Duties collected from October, 1765, to October,
1766, reflect the same decline:[20]

Foreign Sugars	£ 30.	1.	10½
Foreign Molasses	133.	8.	9
King's Share of Fines, Forfeitures & Seizures	32.	11.	2
Gross Receipts	£196.	1.	9½

During Peter Harrison's first year at the Customs House only
£125.0.9 were taken in for duties and fines combined. Against
this total he had to list the following operating charges:

Established and Incidental Salaries	£110.	0.	0
Waiters and Preventive Officers	25.	0.	0
Tidesmen	14.	4.	0
Gauging	7.	1.	0
Weighing	4.	2.	0
Printing	6.	8.	0
Postage	6.	0.	4½
Office Rent	10.	0.	0
Firewood	6.	0.	0
Other Articles	42.	17.	10¾
Total	£233.	13.	3¼

18. *Connecticut Colonial Records*, 14, pp. 486, 498; Birket, *Some Cursory Remarks*, 36; Carl Bridenbaugh, ed., Patrick M'Robert, *A Tour through Part of the North Provinces of America...in the Years 1774 and 1775* (Philadelphia, 1935), 12; Lawrence H. Gipson, *Jared Ingersoll* (New Haven, 1920), 16-34.
19. District of New Haven, Foreigners Inward, 1765-66.
20. Duties Collected in America by the American Commissioners of Customs,

Although the addition of the Collector's salary and some incidentals made these expenses £69.6.8¾ greater than those of the
previous year, the "Charges of Management exceeding the produce" were actually less by £42.3.4¼.[21] The improvement can be
explained by the activity of the officers in making seizures and in
levying fines for violation of the law. In the latter respect, where
his brother had been popularly lax, Peter proceeded with real
vigor.[22]

Any way one viewed it, the collectorship with declining fees
and a salary of only £60 a year was not much of a post. On the
other hand it did not require much attention once Harrison had
it properly organized under the efficient George Mills and his sub-
ordinates, and at least until 1773 the New Haven customs office
ran smoothly.[23] There was more than a little truth in Joseph Har-

Oct. 10, 1765-Oct. 10, 1766, Treasury 1: Bundle 442, ff. 30-31, Library of Congress
Transcripts; A. O., Declared Accounts, Bundle 822, Roll 1072.

21. Consult the "Pitkin Papers," Connecticut Historical Society, *Collections*,
19 (1920), pp. 97-98, for New Haven Customs Revenues for 1766-1767; and
Treasury 1: Bundle 442, ff. 30-31, for 1765-1766. For seizures and fines, see A. O.,
Declared Accounts, Bundle 483, Roll 1134, Transcripts in Massachusetts Historical
Society.

22. A. O., Declared Accounts, Bundle 483, Roll 1134. See Table, p. 146, in the
present work.

23. The Customs House routine may be summarized as follows:
   I. *Indoor Business*
      A. In relation to exporting: 1) receiving the invoice of the goods and
         comparing it with the records of the out-of-doors officers who super-
         vised the lading; 2) taking bonds for lumber and non-enumerated
         commodities, giving and cancelling certificates; 3) hearing oaths and
         giving a certificate that goods on which bounties would be paid in
         England were of North-American production and would be taken
         directly to England; 4) examining the certificates of masters who
         had given bond at an English port; and 5) collecting duties on certain
         exports.
      B. In relation to importing: 1) receiving the manifests and reports,
         giving warrant for unloading goods, and taking the master's oath as
         to the truth of his statements; 2) collecting duties on imports accord-
         ing to law, which at New Haven fell largely under the laws of 6
         George III, 6 George II, and 4 George III.

rison's claim made many years later to Sir Grey Cooper of the Treasury, "I had a Brother, whose abilities and accomplishments, would have done credit to an office of much more importance, than a small American Collectorship; but it so happened that he never had the good fortune to get any higher preferment than to be Collector of New Haven in Connecticut." [24]

At fifty years of age Peter Harrison was in the prime of life, even though his health was not of the best, and he was hardly disposed to regard his post as a mere sinecure. His conciliatory nature, however, led him to endeavor to make the strict enforcement of the revenue laws as palatable to fair traders as possible. A situation arose early in 1768 that faced him and his fellow officials in Connecticut with a real dilemma. The Townshend Acts of 1767 had legalized the use of Writs of Assistance for the suppression of smuggling, and the American Board of Customs Commissioners instructed Harrison to apply to the "Superior, or Supreme Court of your Province, who are empowered by the said Act to grant the same." [25] Duncan Stewart and Dr. Thomas Moffatt, collector and comptroller at New London, also applied for the search warrants and forwarded their applications to Harrison for presentation

---

C. Keeping accounts and sending copies in various forms to the cashier, the comptroller, the Treasury, and the Inspector of Imports and Exports, as well as swearing to the accounts before the governor.
D. Corresponding with the above offices, with the Board of Customs Commissioners at Boston, officers in other ports, and on occasion with English agents in foreign ports.
E. Registering ships or examining registers.
F. Collecting 6d. duty for Greenwich Hospital.
II. *Outdoor Business*
A. Supervising the out-of-doors officers.
B. Searching and seizing.
C. Prosecuting for violations of the law.
This summary was prepared for me by Professor Dora Mae Clark.
24. Joseph Harrison to Sir Grey Cooper, April 10, 1778, A. O. 13: Bundle 41.
25. Treasury 1: Bundle 465.

with his own at the court's New Haven sitting. The New Haven application, submitted on February 23, 1768, read as follows:

Honble Gentlemen,

In consequence of an Act passed last Session of Parliament, authorising and directing you to grant Writs of Assistants to Customs house Officers within your Jurisdiction, and in Compliance with Order received from the Honble Board of Customs Commissioners at Boston, we take this opportunity to apply to you for the same.

We are very respectfully, &c.
PETER HARRISON
GEORGE MILLS [26]

What followed was of great import to all courts in America as well as to the Customs Officers. Peter Harrison stated the case of the King's officials in a report to the American Board at Boston, written on March 2:

In obedience to Your Orders to us of 11th January, we have applied to the Judges of the Superior Court for Writs of Assistance by Letter of which the Inclosed is a Copy. It was delivered by Mr. [Jared] Ingersoll, an eminent Lawyer of this Place on the first day of the Court. When the time of the Courts breaking up drew near he informed us, that the Judges had read the Letter in his hearing immediately after he presented it, and from what conversation then past, he had reason to think, that they were not at this time disposed to comply with it. We instructed Mr. Ingersoll to signify to them our desire of a reply in writing. This he informed us he likewise did, but the Court broke up and we have received none. The Deputy Governor [Jonathan Trumbull] who is also Chief Judge in a private Conversation hinted to us the principal reasons of their non-compliance that they were not clear that the thing was in it self constitutional, they were strangers to every Mode of Application besides Petition, nor did it avail when we informed him that we were confined to the Mode which we had adopted.

We consider it our duty to inform you of this matter as soon as possible.[27]

26. Treasury 1: Bundle 491, p. 45.
27. *Ibid.*, Bundle 491, p. 44.

Since the judges conveniently made no determination at New Haven, Stewart and Moffatt filed a formal petition when the Court sat at Norwich on March 28. No action was taken.[28] A year later the New London officials again renewed their application and their attorney, Thomas Seymour, requested a "Judicial Determination" of the matter. Believing the Parliamentary act authorizing writs to be unconstitutional, Chief Justice Trumbull had earlier sought the opinion of the General Assembly and had been advised that judgment lay with the Court, although privately several members urged him not to grant the writs. Many in Connecticut feared the loss of the charter should the Court prove adamant. The judges delayed, however, and no writs were ever issued. Trumbull wrote to William Samuel Johnson, Connecticut's agent in England, explaining his position:

I have taken care to find what the Courts in other Colonies have done, and find that no such Writs have been given by any of the Courts except in Massachusetts and New Hampshire, where they were given as soon as asked for. I believe the Courts in all the other Colonies will be as well united, and as firm in this Matter, as in anything that has yet happened between us and Great Britain.[29]

Fortunately for Peter Harrison he had settled at New Haven while the community was passing through a conservative reaction to the lawlessness of the Stamp Act agitation. Moreover the new official was promptly and cordially received into the company of the friends of Joseph, who had left Connecticut in good repute. Sage advice from Jared Ingersoll doubtless forestalled any second

28. Treasury 1: Bundle 491, p. 214.
29. I. W. Stuart, *Life of Jonathan Trumbull* (Boston, 1859), 80-81. On the question of writs in general consult Emily Hickman, "Colonial Writs of Assistance," *New England Quarterly*, 5 (1932), 83-104; Oliver M. Dickerson, "Writs of Assistance as a Cause of the Revolution," Richard B. Morris, ed., *The Era of the American Revolution* (New York, 1939), 52-55; and Josiah Quincy, Jr., *Reports of Cases . . . in the Superior Court of . . . Massachusetts* (Boston, 1865), 501-504.

application for writs by Harrison, especially since New London was the more important customs district and any decision handed down to Stewart and Moffatt would cover New Haven as well. Even though he had thus avoided an open breach, beneath the surface a strong tide of animosity was running against all customs officers because of the strict enforcement of the new revenue laws. The situation for Peter was rendered all the more critical by news emanating from Massachusetts that on June 10, 1768, his brother Joseph, now collector of the port of Boston, had seized John Hancock's sloop *Liberty* on a suspicion of smuggling and had, with his son Richard Acklam Harrison, received very rough treatment from a waterfront mob managed by Samuel Adams.[30] That the officer who seized John Hancock's vessel, and who was rumored to have instigated the whole affair, was his brother did Peter Harrison no good and gave him little peace at New Haven coming so shortly after the difficulty over the Writs of Assistance.

Easier times seemed about to settle over the customs house on Long Wharf when the unpopular George Mills, who played "most agreeably on his Violin," left to become Inspector of the Customs in the Southern Provinces. The *Connecticut Journal*, sneering at his "sociability and personal Accomplishments" which "had gained him nameless friendly Offices," regarded his departure as

---

30. Joseph Harrison was badly "bruised, particularly in the breast," and Richard Acklam Harrison was dragged by his hair some distance until someone rescued him from the mob. The rioters burned the Collector's pleasure boat (which he had built himself) and broke all the windows of his house on the Common. Yet even so prominent a radical leader as William Molineux promptly wrote to Harrison "to be Assur'd that the Town in General have the same Good Disposition your merit Claims," and regretted "the severe treatment you have no ways merited." The elder brother never recovered from the physical beating he received in this fracas. Seventy-Six Society, *Papers Relating to the Public Events in Massachusetts preceding the American Revolution*, 63-64, 67, 73, 75; Chalmers Papers, III, 2, 3, in Sparks Manuscripts, X, Houghton Library, Harvard University. See also an excellent account by George W. Wolkins, "The Seizure of John Hancock's Sloop Liberty," Massachusetts Historical Society, *Proceedings*, 55 (1923), 239-84.

a good riddance although there was no rejoicing over the appointment of a local Tory, Christopher Kilby, as his successor.[31] All might have gone well had Peter not involved himself in a religious squabble about the same time Joseph seized the sloop *Liberty*.

Among his Connecticut acquaintances was the Reverend Samuel Peters, rector of the Anglican Church at Hebron, who still claims the attention of posterity as the fabricator of the infamous "Blue Laws." This "hot-church Tory" amply revenged himself upon the sons of the Sons of Liberty for a mobbing of 1774 by composing that strange and fascinating mosaic of fact, fancy, and falsehood, *A General History of Connecticut* (1781), the conscious mockery of which has ever since plagued humorless historians of the Nutmeg State. In this book the parson tells a heroic tale about Peter Harrison.

It seems that one of the founders of New Haven, Thomas Grigson (Gregson), tiring of life among the Lords Brethren, and, before sailing off to England in the famous "Phantom Ship" in 1644, made out a will bequeathing his property "towards the support of an episcopal clergyman, who should reside in that Town." He was lost at sea with the whole ship's company, but a friend proved and recorded his will. Scandalized by the terms of the bequest the honest selectmen glued together the pages of the record book where the will was copied and promptly sold the land for taxes. When, in 1750, an Episcopal clergyman first settled at New Haven, the Gregson gift was remembered but no churchman was permitted to search the records for it. At this point let Mr. Peters tell his own story:

In 1768, Peter Harrison, Esq. from [Bawtry,] Nottinghamshire, in England, the King's collector at the port of Newhaven, claimed his right of searching the public records; and, being a stranger, and not supposed

31. *Connecticut Journal,* May 20, 1768.

to have any knowledge of Grigson's will, obtained his demand. The alphabet contained Grigson's name, and referred to a page which was not to be found in the book. Mr. Harrison at first supposed it to have been torn out; but, on a closer examination, discovered one leaf much thicker than the others. He put a corner of the thick leaf in his mouth, and soon found it was composed of two leaves, which with much difficulty having separated, he found Grigson's will! To make sure he took a copy of it himself, and then called the clerk to draw and attest another; which was done. Thus furnished, Mr. Harrison instantly applied to the selectmen, and demanded a surrender of the land which belonged to the church, but which they as promptly refused; whereupon Mr. Harrison took out writs of ejectment against the possessors. As might be expected, Mr. Harrison, from a good man, became, in ten days, the worst man in the world; but, being a generous and brave Englishman, he valued not their clamours and curses, though they terrified the gentlemen of the law. Harrison was obliged to be his own lawyer, and boldly declared he expected to lose his cause in New-England; but after that he would appeal, and try it, at his own expence, in Old England, where justice reigned. The good people, knowing Harrison did not get his bread by their votes, and that they could not baffle him, resigned the lands to the church on that gentleman's own terms; which in a few years will support a clergyman in a very genteel manner.[32]

In this romantic recital there is just enough fact to give the episode some foundation. While he was in London taking orders in the Church, Jonathan Arnold obtained on March 26, 1735, from William Gregson, great-grandson of Thomas, an indenture conveying to him one and three quarters acres of land at the corner of what are now Church and Chapel Streets to be held for building a church. Upon his return to New Haven in 1736 Arnold found others occupying the land and did not take legal steps for recovery until September 6, 1738, when a true copy of the deed was recorded in the New Haven Land Records. When he attempted to

32. Samuel Peters, *A General History of Connecticut* (2d edn., London, 1782), 189-93.

take possession he was set upon by a "mob," consisting largely of Yale students, and driven off.[33]

The records of the formation of Trinity Parish, New Haven, have long since disappeared. Although there was clearly a claim in equity under the Gregson deed, Anglicans were debarred from the property in 1752 when Samuel Mix conveyed a piece of land on the opposite corner of the New Haven Green to Enos Alling and Isaac Doolittle for the use of the church. In November, 1765, Alling did purchase the Gregson tract by "warranty deed" and conveyed it to the vestry. Because the title had been in dispute since 1647, and, by both the English and Connecticut laws of inheritance, William Gregson could have asserted his claim, William Samuel Johnson, Connecticut agent at London, was instructed by the vestry to extinguish the Gregson claim forever. He was successful in this undertaking, and on October 26, 1768, sent a deed of release to Trinity Church.

Fourteen years elapsed before this deed was recorded at New Haven. It seems highly probable that such steps as Peter Harrison actually took were to hasten the recording of the deed by the town authorities, for at this moment the controversy over the possibility of the appointment of an Anglican bishop for the colonies was raging in Connecticut with a bitterness and an intensity that only religious strife can engender. Whatever his actions were, it is

33. On November 3, 1738, the Reverend Samuel Johnson wrote to England: "Mr. Arnold is well. . . . He also meets with very injurious Treatment from the people of New Haven, where one Mr. Gregson of London gave him a lot of land to build a church on, which had descended to him from an ancestor of his who was one of the first settlers of that Town. Mr. Arnold went the other day to take possession of it, and was allowed, without molestation from the person who had it in possession, to enter upon it, and ploughed in it till afternoon, when he was mobbed off by one hundred and fifty people." Writing in 1768, the Reverend Charles Inglis accused William Livingston, stout opponent of an Anglican Episcopate in the colonies, of having been among the Yale students present. For a detailed account, see E. E. Beardsley, *The History of the Episcopal Church in Connecticut* (New York, 1869), I, 113-14, 114n., 168-69, 224-27.

certain that they detracted from his popularity with the Congregationalist element who made up the overwhelming majority of the town's population.

The fast-moving events of 1768 proved too difficult for even the mild and affable Peter Harrison to circumvent. For the first time since his marriage he was in trouble. To say that he was frightened is an understatement, for, considering his brother's fate and his own problems, how could he have felt otherwise? Jared Ingersoll and Enos Alling, his best friends at New Haven, were also suspect. The former architect had now to pay the penalty of conviction and place as his hitherto fair reputation suffered a partial eclipse, making his departure from town both desirable and imperative until the storm blew over.

A trip to Boston for consultation with the Board of Customs Commissioners about the New Haven situation provided the Collector with a plausible excuse for quitting the town until the community temper cooled off.[34] The actual date of this flight is uncertain, but it was probably early in 1769. After visiting Dr. Thomas Moffatt at New London, he traveled to Newport to inspect his estate, and was there long enough to inspire a local hatter, Jacob Barney, to try to collect an old debt. The warrant, sworn out in the March court for £18 lawful money owed "by the Book," described the defendant as of "Boston in the County of Suffolk," but because Sheriff Lillibridge could find "neither Body

34. We can imagine the feelings of the Collector when, in May, 1768, the Connecticut Assembly passed an act to lay duties on goods imported by persons not inhabitants of the colony, and allowed its own appointees ten per cent of the revenue. In April, 1769, during Harrison's absence, the New Haven Town Meeting chose Colonel David Wooster to be collector. The law, be it noted, was directed principally against the competition of New York traders who undersold local merchants and drained the colony of specie. J. H. Trumbull and C. J. Hoadly, eds., *Public Records of the Colony of Connecticut* (Hartford, 1850-90), 13, pp. 72, 74; New Haven Town Records, 1684-1769, under date of April 10, 1769; A. O., Declared Accounts, Bundle 483, Roll 1134.

nor Estate . . . by Reason this Execution came to Hand too late," the warrant was never served.[35] Harrison had gone on his way.

Reaching Boston, Peter found Joseph still carrying on his work at the Customs House, although obviously without his wonted energy and enthusiasm. He told Peter of the "universal detestation" of the revenue service in Massachusetts, "where the whole Country are determined to evade" it. Smuggling frowned on eighteen months ago is now openly encouraged. Fees have fallen off by half, and "extra official duty and employments" are increasing because the Commissioners are using him as a "Shield to catch all the Darts of Resentment pointed against their management." [36]

The brothers found some solace in Joseph's scientific interests. The renown that Peter and Joseph Harrison had achieved in architecture, engineering, and natural philosophy had brought them intercolonial recognition. On April 1, 1768, they had been elected to membership in the American Society, held at Philadelphia, for Promoting Useful Knowledge, which, by merging with a rival body, had been transformed into the American Philosophical Society by the time Peter reached Boston.[37] James Bowdoin sought the assistance of "the Rhode Island Engineer" and his brother in February, 1769, in connection with the expedition Professor John Winthrop of Harvard College was fitting out to observe the transit of Venus at Newfoundland. The astronomer had heard that Joseph Harrison owned an astronomical instrument which "he might probably be willing to lend upon such an occa-

35. Harrison defaulted and on May 25, 1771, the plaintiff was awarded £9.3.6. Inferior Court of Common Pleas, Book H.

36. John Wentworth to Lord Rockingham, November 13, 1768, Wentworth Letter Book, I, 149-50, typescript copy in New Hampshire Historical Society, Concord.

37. The Harrisons were listed as Rhode Island members along with Stephen Hopkins and Ezra Stiles. American Philosophical Society, *Transactions*, I (1771), x-xi; Bridenbaugh, *Rebels and Gentlemen*, 334-39.

sion." [38] Most prized of all Joseph's possessions was this imported quadrant "of Three Feet and a half Radius, with Telescopic Sights, and mounted on a grand Pedestal with a curious Apparatus of Wheelwork to adjust its Motions." It was worth at least one hundred guineas, "and was the more valuable on account of its having been the Property of the Great Astronomer, the late Dr. [Edmund] Halley, and the Instrument with which he made many of his Observations." [39] Joseph generously offered to lend his precious quadrant to a fellow-member in the interest of the great project sponsored by the American Philosophical Society, but Winthrop succeeded in procuring one more suitable for carrying into the wilds.

For nearly two years Governor John Wentworth had been urging Joseph Harrison to visit him at Portsmouth. He played on mutual Yorkshire connections. "We make a Lillipution Wentworth House here; My Domestics mostly Yorkish: and some from W. But to resemble the Original Essentially, We endeavor to make Evry one as happy as we can. I wish to see you exceedingly." Joseph's poor health and the need for a change of scene, as well as a desire to talk over the political situation, and the lure of "a dry bed, remarkably good Air, plain simple Plenty, and the heartiest Welcome in the World" from the first gentleman of New Hampshire led the two discouraged brothers to visit Portsmouth in April.[40]

They found the youthful governor eagerly laying plans for two

38. *Bowdoin and Temple Papers*, I, 116, 119, 120, 127, 129.

39. After more than a year's search the brothers located a microscope for Friend Moses Brown at the Boston shop of "the late Mr. Condy," and sent it with a gift set of Baker's two volumes on the use of the instrument to Providence by "Sabin the carrier" in February, 1769. Testimony of Richard Hallowell, A. O. 13: f. 46; Moses Brown Papers, I, 84, 90, 91, 92, Rhode Island Historical Society.

40. Wentworth House, in Yorkshire, was one of the great show-places of England. John Wentworth to Joseph Harrison, Portsmouth, July 27, 1767; Feb. 13, 1768, Wentworth Letter Book, I, 23-24, 77-78.

interrelated projects. There was much "talk about the state of the Church of England," the nature of which Wentworth later summed up in a letter of September 24. Inasmuch as New Hampshire dissenters "are in very many places broke to pieces by sects, . . ." he explained, "this is the time, which once passed may never again be recovered: but to embrace this opportunity requires caution, prudence, and secrecy." If a governor's chaplain supported by the King were to be sent over to New Hampshire, he could propagate the faith and win over those who "believe there is not any material difference between the Church of England and the Church of Rome," and within two years have a parish of over five hundred people. "By this means I believe the Church would spread fast in New England, and most certainly would produce very desirable effects in the administration of the civil government." [41] That these words thrilled a member of the Society for the Propagation of the Gospel like Joseph Harrison there can be no doubt.

The center of the new parish was to be at Wolfeborough, where on a hill overlooking a small lake near Winnipesaukee, the Governor had begun the foundations of a mansion which he aspired to make far more than a "Lilliputian Wentworth House." In conveying the compliments of his kinsman Michael Wentworth to the Harrisons, their host mentioned the enthusiastic encouragement this Yorkshireman had given to his plans for the Wolfeborough estate: "He is . . . American in *thout*, *Word* and *Work*; instead of Courts and European Magnificence, He talks of Agriculture and American Cultivation, Cutting Vistoes, opening Water Views, and increasing Cattle, and [assures me that I] will soon have a good Farm." [42] As Wentworth asked Peter's advice about planning the

41. John Wentworth to Joseph Harrison, Portsmouth, Sept. 24, 1769, Wentworth Letter Book, I, 288-92.

42. John Wentworth to Joseph Harrison, Portsmouth, Feb. 13, 1768; Sept. 24, 1769, *ibid.*, I, 78, 288.

new house, and perhaps about the kind of chapel that should be erected in the projected parish, the older man's spirits rose and both must have regretted that it was too early in the season to push through the woods for a view of the foundations which were already under construction. But the Governor promised to send careful measurements to Peter as soon as possible.

In addition to planning for the future of the Church of England in New Hampshire, the Wentworths, Atkinsons, and Whipples sought to revive the flagging spirits of their old friends the Harrisons. On May 1, 1769, Governor Wentworth issued as a royal grant of George III a charter for a new town in the province to be called Trecothick after his fellow-Anglican, the alderman of London and agent for New Hampshire. The 24,957 acres were divided into ninety-two equal shares and distributed "unto our loving Subjects Inhabitants of our said Province of New Hampshire and other governments," all of whom were Wentworth's personal friends: "Joseph Harrison, Esqr. of Boston," and "Peter Harrison, Esqr. of New London," Nathaniel Hurd, silversmith of Boston, and Barlow Trecothick of London were the only proprietors not residents of New Hampshire. The grant was made subject to the usual conditions: that a "road for Carriages" be opened through the town; that twelve families be settled by March 1, 1771, and sixty by March 1, 1776; that all white pine trees suitable for masts be preserved for the Navy; that an annual quit rent of one ear of Indian corn be paid on demand.[43]

Had the colony's surveyors set out deliberately to locate the least desirable tract of land in New Hampshire they would inevitably have selected Trecothick. Situated in the central part of the province, this grant was little more than a mountain of the granite that

43. The charter is in the Ellsworth (Trecothick) Town Records, 1-6, Secretary of State's Office, Concord; and is printed less accurately in *New Hampshire State Papers: Town Charters*, 25 (1894), pp. 718-21.

has made New Hampshire famous. It mattered little that in the first division of sixty acres for each proprietor Peter had drawn Lot Number 4 in the Fifth Range, and Joseph Lot Number 2 in the Ninth Range, or that they paid a proprietary tax of three Spanish dollars for their shares in the "Common and undivided lands." Trecothick was not settled before 1776 and the grant lapsed; Ellsworth, as it is now named, is one of the most sparsely settled towns in the state.[44]

When the land grant was made Peter Harrison was down at New London preparing to return to his post and visiting with Dr. Moffatt. There he learned, if he had not already read of it in the newspapers, that Connecticut Anglicans were receiving short shrift at the hands of Congregationalists.[45] Nevertheless, he went back to New Haven and took his responsibilities seriously. Yet this and other considerations increased his apprehension, because on August 23, in the presence of Comptroller Kilby and Colonel Nathaniel Whiting, "persons of fame and reputation," he executed a power of attorney authorizing Ralph Inman of Cambridge, Massachusetts, "to receive from the cashier and paymaster of His Majesty's Customs in America" all salaries and fees due him.[46]

In their discussions of the uncertain future facing them, the brothers apparently had decided to seek safety, redress, and perhaps preferment in the mother country. Although the Customs Commissioners in England had awarded Joseph Harrison £500 sterling as "Compensation for his sufferings and losses" in the *Liberty* affair, his health and spirit were broken. When James Otis referred to him in the *Boston Gazette* as "too contemptible in my opinion to

44. Ellsworth Town Records, 15, 38, 68; Hamilton Child, *Gazetteer of Grafton County, New Hampshire* (Syracuse, 1886), 241.
45. *Connecticut Journal*, June 12, 1769.
46. The power of attorney was made out on August 1, witnessed on August 23, and filed at Boston on November 3, 1769. Registry of Deeds, Suffolk County, Vol. 115, pp. 246-47.

take any further notice of at present, than to declare, that I think him if not a wicked, yet a very weak old man," the Collector realized that his usefulness was at an end.[47] On Sunday, October 8, 1769, Joseph Harrison left forever the land he had chosen for his own and served so well.[48]

This was the time, if ever, for Peter Harrison to have moved; events were inexorably closing in. Ultimately he decided to remain at New Haven as tension between England and her colonies eased towards 1770. Unlike his brother, who had never really put his roots down, Peter was thoroughly acclimated to New England. He felt no burning desire to cross the Atlantic and leave his family and property behind, and besides, Joseph could look after their mutual interests in London as he had always done.

So far as is known, Peter did not go to Boston to bid his brother farewell. The King's officers at New Haven were in for difficult times, and the presence of the collector was imperative. In September the populace had dealt roughly with Nathan Smith, an informer, who several months previously had lodged "a regular information in the Customs House," against "one of the first mer-

47. *Boston Gazette*, Sept. 4, 1769.
48. At London, during 1770-1772, Joseph Harrison again became a man of consequence, giving advice on American conditions and aiding Godfrey Malbone in securing the support of the S. P. G. for a new church at Pomfret, Connecticut. When Thomas Hutchinson's son came over Harrison saw that he was introduced to the right people. In time Harrison went into trade at Liverpool as an associate of Joseph Manesty, but his injuries proved so "troublesome" that his head ached continually when he tried to write. In 1778 he retired to the Acklam estate at Bawtry, where he lived quietly with his family until his death on January 15, 1787. His son, Richard Acklam Harrison, was deputized to his father's position at Boston in 1770. In 1775 he fled to England, where from 1777 to his death *ca.* 1818 he served as collector of the port of Hull. *Bowdoin and Temple Papers*, I, 191, 216; F. L. Hawks and W. S. Perry, eds., *Documentary History of the Protestant Episcopal Church in the United States* (New York, 1863-64), II, 166; Massachusetts Archives, XXII, 333; Loyalist Transcripts, III, 254, New York Public Library; Family Tree, Van Buren Papers; Rowe, *Diary*, 193.

chants in this place," for a breach of the acts of trade as well as for smuggling, and, reported the *Connecticut Journal*, "thereof falsely gave such assurance, as caused the collector much trouble and fruitless expense." The merchant, rowdy Benedict Arnold, forthwith had Smith tarred, feathered, and perched on a stand in the Market Place for all to view and take due warning. A few weeks thereafter Adonijah Thomas was forced to publish an apology in the same newspaper for attempting to inform at the Customs House against Timothy Jones, Jr., "for running of Goods." [49]

Collector Harrison was circumspect and carefully avoided any open rupture with Arnold and his group of smugglers. Nor had he yet become a discouraged and beaten Tory like his brother. In fact, he proceeded against illicit traders with renewed vigor as the sums collected for "Fines and Seizures" abundantly indicate:

1768, Jan. 5–1769, Jan. 5	£ 72. 14. 8½
1769, Jan. 5–1770, Jan. 5	277. 12. 2
1770, Jan. 5–1771, Jan. 5	232. 8. 11
1771, Jan. 5–1772, Jan. 5	350. 10. 3
1772, Jan. 5–1773, Jan. 5	185. 12. 5

This active enforcement of the revenue laws may account in large part for the decline in normal customs receipts after 1770 at New Haven.[50]

As soon as business at the Customs House permitted, Peter Harrison worked on the designs for Wentworth House. In a farewell letter of September 24, 1769, because he was uncertain of Peter's whereabouts, Governor Wentworth had advised Joseph that

Inclos'd are the measurements of my house, wch is now in such a State that it may be divided any way the Architect shall design; as I've only

49. *Connecticut Journal*, Sept. 15, 22, 1769; *Connecticut Courant*, Sept. 15, 1769; *Boston Weekly News-Letter*, Oct. 5, 1769.
50. A. O., Declared Accounts, Bundle 483, Roll 1134; *Connecticut Colonial Records*, 14, p. 498.

One Chimney built in the So. East End and two rooms finish'd with lath and plaister; which I had rather undo, than spoil the House; wch I propose to have as good a habitable House, wth at least one room of forty feet long and proportion[able?] Breadth, as can be contriv'd. This I am sure will be effected by your Brother's Aid.[51]

In 1768 John Wentworth had begun the construction of his "English country seat" on a small plain about one hundred rods east of the lovely lake that now bears his name. Wentworth House was a two-storied frame structure with a gambrel roof and a great central hall opening to both the east and the west. (Figure 13) Whether Peter Harrison required any changes in construction in conformity with his designs is not known, but work progressed and the family was able to occupy it in 1770. On October 4, Frances Wentworth, the Governor's wife, wrote to a friend: "The great dancing room is nearly completed, with the Drawing Room, and begins to make a very Pretty appearance." (Figure 14) The principal room on the upper story, which was eighteen feet in height, was known as the "East India Chamber," probably on account of its decorations which included an India wallpaper and a white marble fireplace with niches on either side for statues. If Harrison's plans had not been forestalled by the Revolution, John Wentworth's estate might have rivalled William Byrd's Westover which had so excited the young governor's admiration during a visit in 1767.[52]

If this undertaking was a reminder of the palmy days at Newport, another echo of the past was less agreeable. After long drawn-

51. John Wentworth to Joseph Harrison, Sept. 24, 1769, Wentworth Letter Book, I, 286-87.
52. The heavy granite foundations are clearly visible today and are proof that an elegant structure was contemplated. The site would have been almost without parallel in colonial America had the "vistoes" and "Water Views" ever been opened. For a few details, see Benjamin F. Parker, *History of Wolfeborough* (Wolfeborough, 1901), 80-84, 85, 88, 92.

out negotiations Harrison found it necessary in November to sue Philip Barzil of Newport, "Fisherman alias Labourer," in an action of trespass and ejectment wherein he demanded recovery of possession of a dwelling adjoining his wife's land at Newport and damages of £50. The Court awarded him possession, damages, and costs of fourteen shillings, three pence, in May, 1771, and the Collector was satisfied. Yet it should not be taken amiss, if we inquire at this point into the feelings of George Rome about £276.14.10 he had lent to Peter Harrison before he moved away from Newport, or the thoughts of John Freebody concerning the loan of £4,000 to the brothers in 1748. (Figure 9) No settlement on the principal of the latter had been made when Joseph departed for England, although he did pay the interest through 1769.[53]

As the routine at the Customs House was perfected, and as receipts continued to shrink after 1772, the Collector left most of the business to Benjamin Sandford who, for a fee, regularly drew up and signed the account. Small sums were expended in 1770 and 1771 for incidentals, but operational expenses were kept down. The fact that Peter Harrison received no salary payment from September 8, 1767, until October 10, 1772, when a payment of £304 was made, supplies an interesting commentary on eighteenth-century governmental procedure.[54] It is clear that only a gentleman with an assured independent income could afford to work for the Customs, unless the fees of the port were ample enough to provide him with a living. This being the case, no censure of Harrison is intended when we say of him that after 1773 "he did nothing in particular and did it very well."

53. Inferior Court of Common Pleas, Book H, p. 619; Note of Peter and Joseph Harrison to John Freebody, June 26, 1749, Newport Historical Society, Autographs, no. 1199; A. O. 13: Bundle 41.

54. A. O., Declared Accounts, Customs, Bundle 824, Rolls 1076-77; Treasury Board Papers, Bundle 482, no. 222, Public Record Office; Testimony of Charles Chauncy, Van Buren Papers.

When Judge Jared Ingersoll announced his intention of renting his "House and Homestead" along with his Mill Lane pasture in 1771, Peter Harrison agreed "to lease" it for one year from May 1, at £38 lawful money, with the understanding that he should pay the taxes and "maintain the Glass and fences in repair." [55] There he established his wife Elizabeth and the children, Hermione, Thomas, Isabelle, and Elizabeth, who were fast growing up.

At twenty-one, Thomas aroused his father's pride because he displayed a real talent at drawing. Whether he was trained in England or America is not known, but a letter to his father in 1771, probably written from Newport, reveals his interest in art:

Sir,

I received the honour of your Letter of the 14 inst. In which you acquaint me that you have Received the Drawings I took the Liberty to send you, which I have the pleasure to find has not proved inexceptable.

I am very sorry I cannot sufficiently explain the particulars you desired as I could wish. The two Round drawings are exact Copys of the Original Etchings of the Celebrated Monsieur Pinell; the Largest is a View of the Harbour of Naples, the other the Plan not mentioned; the view of the Rhine is a copy of an engraving of Muller, the Plan not mentioned. [56]

He closed by expressing the hope of seeing his father at New Haven in the coming spring or summer, and also "by that Time to do myself the pleasure of Presenting you with some Drawings more worthy of your acceptance." Thomas Harrison was also avidly interested in current politics. In June, 1772, when he wrote from New Haven to his chum John Shearman of Newport, that the recent burning of the revenue schooner *Gaspee* near Providence was an insult to the Crown, he echoed an old family conviction by averring that the Rhode Island "Charter must goe. I

55. The Harrisons must have moved to another house by September 12, 1772, when the rent had been paid and all accounts settled. Lease in Jared Ingersoll Papers, New Haven Colony Historical Society.

56. An original draft, undated but probably 1771, Van Buren Papers.

am extreamly glad (and so must [be] every well-wisher of the Colony)." [57]

The world began to fall around Peter Harrison when his son's promising career was cut short on the threshold of success. The *Connecticut Journal* of November 20, 1772, tells the story in the fulsome obituary style of the time:

Last Sunday evening [November 15] died in the 23rd year of his Age, Mr. Thomas Harrison, the only Son of Peter Harrison, Esq: Collector of His Majesty's Customs in this Town.

A Youth of fine natural Parts and happy Acquirements—of a sweet and aimiable Temper—exemplary, pious, humane and dutiful. He easily distinguished himself by a sober, studious, and peaceable Disposition—studiously avoiding the slippery Paths of Vice, in which too many un-thinking Youths pursue—and chose rather the pleasant Road of Virtue, and with undeviating Steps he walked in the same, which has secured him the Approbation of his God.

Conversant in the Study of the Fine Arts, he laid a Foundation to have done Honor to his Family and to have been useful to the Public.[58]

Thomas Harrison was at this time perhaps the only young man in the colonies whose parents were consciously educating him for an artistic career and his premature death was indeed an irreparable loss to a nascent American culture.

In his two periods of activity in civil architecture, Peter Harrison had designed every kind of public building common to the colonies except a state house and a college. He was approached in 1773 for a plan for the latter. The Reverend Eleazar Wheelock, President of newly-opened Dartmouth College, had contemplated the erection of a noble edifice at Hanover as early as 1771. While Dr. Wheelock was taking the waters at Lebanon Springs, New

57. Thomas Harrison to John Shearman, June 22, 1772, Van Buren Papers.
58. "November 15, 1772. Died—Mr. Thomas Harrison. Buried in the Evening of the 18th of the Same." Trinity Church Records: Parochial Register, 1767-1814, I, 20, at the Parish House, New Haven.

York, in 1772, he met Comfort Sever, a house-carpenter of Still-water, in that province, and anticipating the action of the Trustees, as was his wont, he discussed plans for the new building and requested Sever to prepare a set of designs and send them over to Hanover. He wheedled £500 towards the construction out of the parsimonious New Hampshire House of Representatives in May, 1773, and persuaded a meeting of the Trustees at Portsmouth on June 9 to agree "to enter upon the Building of a great College." [59]

After meeting with the Trustees at Portsmouth, the President immediately wrote to Sever that he had borne him in mind "since I last saw you at the Hot Spring," but certain obstacles have arisen which they must surmount. "I enclose a Sketch of the proposal, given in hast by Governor Wentworth. Which he desired me to send to his friend Mr. Harrison of New Haven, desiring him to give a Plan for the Building of the Same, as they judged the Plan you Sent me would be too expensive." Many others have offered to submit designs, Wheelock added, but I have "told them all I had given you incouragement to take the lead in it." And, he concluded significantly in a postscript, "if you come dont fail to bring a good Plan, as it is altogether uncertain Whether one can be had from Mr. Harrison." [60]

With great craft the educator made doubly certain that Comfort Sever would be accommodated with the commission. On June 15 he sent a "Sketch which his Excellency gave to direct an architect in his Plan" to Captain De Peyster, a friend of the College, to suggest an idea of what was intended and to solicit his aid. But not until June 28, when Sever should have had his second set of plans

---

59. *Documents and Records Relating to the Province of New Hampshire* (Nashua, 1873), 7, p. 323; Eleazar Wheelock, *A Continuation of the Narrative of the Indian Charity School* (Hartford, 1773), 23.

60. E. Wheelock to Comfort Sever, June 9, 1773, Dartmouth College Archives, nos. 773,765; 773,378.

under way, did Wheelock send the following equivocal letter to Peter Harrison:

Sir,

The Trustees of this College in their late Meetg. [June 9!], taking into their Consideration the Growth and great Increase of our Number of Students, agreed that it was Necessary that a large Building should be immediately erected. And with the incouragement of £500 Lawfl. Money generously given by this Province to begin with, they determined to enter upon it, bespeaking and relying upon the aid of piously disposed Friends abroad to enable them to effect the Same. And accordingly I am by their desire entering upon it as fast as may be convenient.

And in order thereto a good Plan for the Building is Necessary. I therefore Sent you by Mr. Evered, one of my pupils, 2 or 3 weeks ago a Sketch of what was needed given by Governr. Wentworth, which I suppose Mr. Evered has likely delivered to you before this Time. I here with enclose a Plan of the Ground given after our Woods fashion, not knowing but it may be of some Advantage to you therein, but I imagin there may be a much greater Advantage by your seeing the Ground yourself, which has also been desired by a Number of Gentlemen, though none of them have yet offrd to be at the whole Expence of it, but as I have lately been informed You are in a broken State of Health, and likely may think of Journeying to Serve that I am in hopes you might be induced to take a Journey here for a less Reward than you would think reasonable if you had no other Motive. If this Should be the Case, Sir, I should greatly rejoyce in the Opportunity to receive the proposed Advantage by You, and Yourself have the Pleasure of Contributing that Service which I doubt not will add much to the Reputation of this benevolent Design. And the Sooner this preliminary be Settled the better. If You should not find it in your way to come Yourself you may transmit the Plan by the Post to the care of the Revd. Mr. Stephen Williams of Springfield, who has frequent Opportunity of Conveye to me.

I am Sir with Sincere Respect and Esteem, though unknown,

Your Friend and Humble Servt.
ELEAZAR WHEELOCK [61]

61. E. Wheelock to Captain De Peyster, June 15, 1773; to Peter Harrison, June 28, 1773, *ibid.*

In view of Peter Harrison's reputation as the foremost colonial architect and the strong advocacy of his friend's case by Dartmouth College's principal patron, one may inquire why the clergyman issued an invitation so patently calculated to elicit a refusal. The answer may very well be found in the Newlight Presbyterianism of Comfort Sever and even more in the Tory Anglicanism of both the Governor and Peter Harrison. The conspiracy of Joseph Harrison and John Wentworth to promote the Church of England in New Hampshire was no secret, and only recently the Governor had tried to wean Tutor Sylvanus Ripley away from the College and Congregationalism by the promise of a place at King's Chapel, if he would take Episcopal orders, and, moreover, Peter Harrison's fame as a designer of churches came from Anglican patronage. For the first time Harrison failed to respond to an appeal for assistance, but since the death of his son, his never robust health had become much worse. Then, too, the President had already made arrangements of his own. Whatever the reasons, the architect never sent any plans from New Haven and there is no answer to Dr. Wheelock's brash letter in the Dartmouth College Archives.

When Dartmouth Hall was eventually built after the Revolutionary War it was only some master-carpenter's crude imitation of Robert Smith's Nassau Hall at Princeton or his College Edifice at Providence. Had it been erected after a design drawn by Peter Harrison, Dartmouth College would have been fortunate in the possession of the outstanding example of pre-revolutionary American college architecture. Who can say, it might even have inaugurated a new style of collegiate building.[62]

62. There is a rejected plan by William Gamble in the Dartmouth College Archives. See also, John Wentworth to E. Wheelock, Jan. 20, 1775, Wentworth Letter Book, III, 49; Frederick Chase, *History of Dartmouth College and the Town of Hanover, New Hampshire* (Hanover, 1891), I, 271, 278; Wheelock, *Narrative* (1773), 23-25; David McClure and Elijah Parish, *Memoirs of the Rev.*

This entire incident provides a concrete explanation of the eclipse of Peter Harrison's fame and status as the foremost colonial architect. His Tory sentiments, his Anglicanism, and his associates had made him *persona non grata* to the Patriots. With the onset of the Revolution his name and works were forgotten, and when the country again had time to consider the elements of taste and architecture, new leaders arose to set the pattern. Thomas Jefferson, as much of a disciple of Palladio as Peter Harrison, independently succeeded in making his innovation the new national style. A revolution in architecture paralleled that in government, and, ironically, it was not the beauty of the classic manner but rather its affinity to the republicanism of the age that commended it to the civic leaders of the new generation.

At New Haven the Harrison family lived a gentle existence. Their home was sumptuously furnished in the best of taste with furniture, books, paintings, and pictures brought down from Newport. In the stable were two fine riding chairs and two horses trained for either driving or riding. When Madam Harrison joined her husband for exercise or travel she frequently rode on a pillion. At home they were faithfully served by two Negro slaves, Lucy and Apollo, who had long been with the family.[63] Hermione, Isabelle, and Elizabeth were beautiful young women and already attracting the attention of local sparks—perhaps even a Yale man or two came to call—but even so nobody could fill the void left by Thomas. Death struck the Harrisons again in 1774, carrying off Isabelle at the age of twenty-two.[64]

At fifty-eight Peter Harrison had become an old man; his health

Eleazar Wheelock, D. D. (Newburyport, 1811), 307-8; New Hampshire Historical Society, *Collections*, 9 (1889), 82.

63. Inventory, Appendix D.
64. Family Tree, Van Buren Papers.

was broken, his purpose in life was gone; and, when he surveyed
the seething political scene in Connecticut, he was terrified. As a
man of property he was too conservative, as an English-born royal
official and self-made gentleman he was too much of an aristocrat
to adjust his ways or to comprehend the significance of a mob that
had begun to think and reason. To continue as a loyal crown officer
and carry out faithfully his duties at the Customs House meant
to court and incur great danger. Peter Harrison's fears were soon
justified.

In 1774 radical New Haven Whigs organized an aggressive
"Committee of the Friends of Constitutional Liberty," which
"Patriotick Club," as Judge Ingersoll termed it, was soon charged
with instigating "mobs, riots, and unjustifiable outrages" against
local Tories. Notwithstanding its emphatic denials, the club thoroughly cowed the Loyalists. Revolution threatened on November
18, 1774, when the Town Meeting voted to enforce the Continental Association and went so far as to appoint a committee to oversee
the adherence of the members of Trinity Church to its extra-legal
revolutionary program of non-intercourse with the mother country.[65]

Contemporary evidence of the activities of the waterfront mob
at New Haven during 1774 and 1775 is strangely lacking, but ten
years later, under oath, Hermione Harrison Cargey told the Loyalist Commissioners at London that her father, "Peter Harrison,
received great abuse and many insults from the Rebels on account
of his Loyalty in the Year 1774 and 1775." To this, Benedict
Arnold, who should have known whereof he spoke, added: "I was
intimately acquainted with the late Peter Harrison, Esq: . . . He
was esteemed a loyal Subject to the British Government, and in
Consequence . . . suffered great abuse from the Americans." Har-

65. Oscar Zeichner, *Connecticut's Years of Controversy* (Chapel Hill, 1949),
176; *Connecticut Courant*, Nov. 21, 1774.

rison's official position plus his robust Anglicanism rendered him especially "obnoxious to the Governor, General Assembly, the protestant dissenting Ministers, and other factions and rebellious spirits," testified the Reverend Samuel Peters.[66]

As he lived through these perilous years Collector Harrison must have often wished that he had gone back to England with Joseph in 1769. A virtual state of war between Whigs and Tories obtained in Connecticut in the early months of 1775. News of actual bloodshed at Lexington and Concord hastened the end of a life that had held so much promise and seen so much accomplishment. His world turned upside down, America's great architect died of a stroke—a "fit" they called it—on April 30, 1775. A week later his remains were interred in the Trinity Church he had courageously stepped forward to defend years before. Because he died intestate an inventory of his estate was made, and, upon posting a bond for £2,000, Elizabeth Pelham Harrison was appointed administrator by the Probate Court.[67]

Three weeks after his death, in the city he had served without stint, Printer Southwick could find space in the *Newport Mercury* only for this brief notice! "Died . . . at New Haven, suddenly, Peter Harrison, Esq:" [68] This was the price of loyalty!

66. A. O. 13: Bundles 41, 68.
67. Trinity Church Records: Parochial Register, I, 33; New Haven Probate Records, XII, 51, Connecticut State Library.
68. *Newport Mercury*, May 29, 1775; *Connecticut Gazette, and Universal Intelligencer*, New London, May 19, 1775.

Epilogue

IN ITS essence the American Revolution was not a revolt against England as such. There was no hypocrisy in colonial protestations of affection for the mother country. The Patriot leaders sought to break through a system from which neither they nor their English rulers had been able to discover a peaceful escape during the years after 1763. The spectacle of naked force being used against Wilkes by King and Parliament seemed a portent of what this system could become when challenged. There was no alternative for those who cherished their liberties. Civil conflict broke out in the colonies because there were Americans—and their numbers were not insignificant—who feared their fellows below them even more than they did the system. First among the victims of Patriot fear and fury were the royal officials of the colonial establishment whom England so signally failed to protect.

By his premature death Peter Harrison was spared the final agony of witnessing the separation. Yet, at New Haven not even the family and property of the dead were immune; loyalty was pursued beyond the grave. Scarcely had the effects of the deceased gentleman been inventoried when the Sons of Liberty took charge. Details of the event, which have been buried for years, are still obscure. Mr. Harrison's Tory friend, Joshua Chandler of New Haven, told the Loyalist Commissioners in 1784 that the Collector's "house and the Customs House was broken open by a Mob; and plundered to a considerable amount." More light is shed on the affair by Mrs. Cargey's description of the scenes of mobbing, which are reminiscent of the treatment of Thomas Hutchinson and the Newport Tories during the Stamp Act riots. She submitted a claim for furniture, clothing, paintings, pictures, "and a large and elegant Library of Books containing to the best of my remembrance between Six and Seven Hundred Volumes, besides Manuscripts and a large Collection of Drawings, all of which were destroyed by a Riotous Mob in 1775." Fortunately, as a postscript to her list of "Particulars lost at Newhaven," Peter's daughter appended the following important clue: "To add, King Seers took away a pair of coach Horses which cost Mr. Harrison £70.0.0."[1]

Isaac Sears, merchant, leader of the Sons of Liberty and New York City's principal agitator, had been rescued by a mob at the prison's door in Manhattan on April 15, 1775, and shortly after fled to New Haven until the affair blew over. There he kept his hand in by joining in the plundering of the Customs House and the Harrison home sometime early in November before, astride one of Peter Harrison's horses, he headed a raid back into New York to deal with the Tory printer, James Rivington.[2] On the wanton mobbing of King Sears and the New Haven Patriots, then, must be placed the blame for the destruction of the priceless designs and engineering drawings of the first American architect. Peter Harrison's buildings are his fitting but only monument.

"To avoid further persecution" Mrs. Harrison and her two daughters sought refuge at her home in Newport. Before the British forces arrived at Rhode Island the Harrisons suffered further

1. A. O. 13: Bundles 41, 68.
2. Sears and his party seized Rivington's types and press on November 23, 1775. *Dict. Amer. Biog.*, XVI, 539-40; Carl L. Becker, *History of Political Parties in the Province of New York, 1760-1776* (Madison, 1909), 245-46.

APPENDICES

APPENDIX A

The Harrison Family Tree

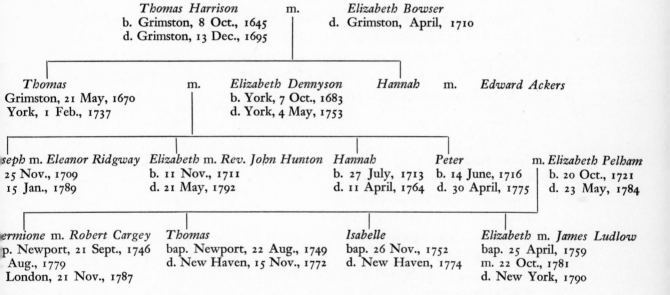

Thomas Harrison　　　　m.　　　　*Elizabeth Bowser*
b. Grimston, 8 Oct., 1645　　　d. Grimston, April, 1710
d. Grimston, 13 Dec., 1695

Thomas　　　　m.　　　　*Elizabeth Dennyson*　　　*Hannah*　　m.　　*Edward Ackers*
Grimston, 21 May, 1670　　b. York, 7 Oct., 1683
York, 1 Feb., 1737　　　　d. York, 4 May, 1753

seph m. *Eleanor Ridgway*　*Elizabeth* m. *Rev. John Hunton*　*Hannah*　　*Peter*　　　m. *Elizabeth Pelham*
25 Nov., 1709　　　　b. 11 Nov., 1711　　　　b. 27 July, 1713　b. 14 June, 1716　b. 20 Oct., 1721
15 Jan., 1789　　　　d. 21 May, 1792　　　　d. 11 April, 1764　d. 30 April, 1775　d. 23 May, 1784

ermione m. *Robert Cargey*　*Thomas*　　　　*Isabelle*　　　*Elizabeth* m. *James Ludlow*
p. Newport, 21 Sept., 1746　bap. Newport, 22 Aug., 1749　bap. 26 Nov., 1752　bap. 25 April, 1759
Aug., 1779　　　　d. New Haven, 15 Nov., 1772　d. New Haven, 1774　m. 22 Oct., 1781
London, 21 Nov., 1787　　　　　　　　　　　　　　　　　d. New York, 1790

APPENDIX B

Peter Harrison's Library (1775)

The following list of books is taken from An Inventory of the Estate of Peter Harrison Esqr. late of New Haven deceased, made on June 28, 1775. The remainder of the inventory is given in Appendices C and D.[1] There were probably more books left at Newport when Harrison went to New Haven. For convenience of reference I have separated the architectural books and placed them in Appendix C.

76 single magazines	@ 2d.	£0.12. 8
82 old do.	@ 1d.	6. 1
Jones' Iron work	1 vol.	7. 6
Leblond's Elements of work		10. –
Thomas [?] on fortifications		15. –
Le Blond's Elements war artillery }		18. –
Do. on Attacks paper cover }		
Johnson's Dictionary	2 vols.	7.10. –
1 Large quarto Bible with Cuts & Maps		3. 0. 0
Moll's Geography	fol.	2. 5. –
Drake's History of York City	do.	2. 0. 0
Marlborough's Wars	do.	1. 0. 0
Hugh's History of Barbadoes	do.	10. –
English Pilot		16. –
Domestic Medicine Wm. Buchan	quarto	6. –

[1] Estate of Peter Harrison, Town of New Haven, 1775, No. 4710, New Haven Probate District, Connecticut State Library, Hartford.

Dyche's Dictionary		£0. 6. –
Johnson	do.	6. –
Every man his own Lawyer		10. –
Ferdinand's Campaigns		1. 0. –
Muller's Artillery		14. 0
Wm. & Amy [sic], Canes Campaign		0. 3. 0
Dalrymple's Memoirs	3 vol.	1. 0. 0
Universal Magazine	9 vol.	1. 7. 0
London Magazine 5	@ 3/	15. 0
Annual Register 5	@ 3/9	18. 9
Douglass Summary		14. –
Vaubaun's Fortification		10. –
Naval Trade & Commerce	2 vol.	4. –
Queen Ann's Reign		2. –
History of Europe	3 vol.	6. 6
Hale's Husbandry	4	1. 5. –
Nelson on Education	1	6. –
Muller Fortification		8. –
Moral & Political Dialogues		2. 6
Lind on hot Climates		6. –
Tissot on health	2 Vol.	6. –
Do. on Literary & Sedentary persons		3. –
Tale of a Tub		3. 9
Cadogan's Essay on nursing		2. 6
Robinson Crusoe	2 Vol.	4. –
Love's Surveying		4. –
Lind on the Scurvy		4. –
Biggs military History		6. –
Gentleman's Farriery		3. –
Partisan		1. 6
Muller's Attack or Fortification		8. –
Common prayer gilt		7. 6
History standing Army in England		1. 0
The strong man armed		1. 0
Gud's miscellany		1. 0
English Dictionary		1. 6
Free mason's Constitutions		1. 0
Ship & Supercargo book keeper		1. 0
History of Spain in Spanish		1. 0

		£	s.	d.
Mair's book keeping		0.	2.	6
Collin's Navigation			1.	—
Treatise on the Teeth			1.	—
Surveyor's desire fulfilled			2.	—
Theory of the Earth			1.	—
Survey of British Customs			16.	—
Improving clayey Grounds			1.	—
7 registers			3.	6
Temple's Miscellany			1.	0
Military & Sea Dictionary			1.	6
Naval Dictionary			1.	0
Description of the Orkney's			1.	0
Puerilia			1.	0
Bailey's Dictionary			3.	—
Homer's Iliads english			.	6
Barrow's industry			.	6
Account of S———berland			1.	6
Masque			1.	6
Compleat Shipwright			1.	0
Braddock's Campaign			1.	0
Muller's Fortification in paste boards			7.	—
Hoyles' Games			2.	—
Atkin's register			1.	—
Gough's Grammar			1.	—
Letter Writer			1.	6
Female War			1.	—
Polite Letters			1.	—
Loughton's Grammar			1.	—
Brown's Catechisms			1.	—
Defence of the female Sex			1.	—
Six Weeks Tour			6.	—
Vicar Wakefield			6.	—
Entick's Dictionary			2.	0
Youth's faithful Monitor			2.	—
Hervey's Meditations	2 Vol		4.	—
Beauties of English Prose			18.	—
Hudibras			4.	—
Hill's family Herbal			2.	—
Polite English Secretary			1.	—

Gordon's Geogral. Grammar		£0. 1. –
Preceptor	2 Vol	10. –
Nature displayed	7 Vol	2. 0. 0
Tour thro' Great Britain	4 Vol	16. –
Beauties of the Spectators	2 Vol	8. –
Modern Europe		1. 6
3 Vol Spectators		4. 6
Love Letters		1. –
M———— Geography		1. –
Familiar Letters		1. –
Piracy & Plunder		1. –
Thoughts on Education		2. –
Female Fables		1. 6
Brown's Catechisms		1. –
Guardian		1. –
The Packet broke open		1. –
Present State Great Britain		1. –
Religion Duke Buckingham		1. –
Fortunate Complaint	/6	. 6
Hutchinson's History Massachusetts		5. –
Herculaneum a pamphlet		4. –
Bouquet's Expedition		2. –
Hill's family Practise		3. –
Institutes of Health		2. –
2 Charts of the Mediterranean		3. –
1 do. of Welch Coast		1. 6
11 Plays		2. 6
Byron's voyage		1. –
41 Pamphlets on various subjects		3. 0.10
44 London Magazines	@ 6d	1. 2. 0

Architectural Works in the Inventory
of Peter Harrison (1775)

This list of books on architecture and construction is taken from the inventory of Harrison's personal property made at New Haven on June 28, 1775, and includes all the works he is known to have used except Batty Langley's *Treasury of Designs*, which he must at one time have possessed. Perhaps it was left behind at Newport. A complete bibliographical reference to the first edition of each work is given below. This and the preceding list of books are not itemized in the inventory copied in the New Haven Probate Records, but they do appear in the original inventory filed in the Connecticut State Library at Hartford.

Gibbs Architecture 2. 0. 0	1 Vol :	James Gibbs, *A Book of Architecture, containing designs of buildings and ornaments* (London, 1728).
Swan's design 2. –. 0	do. :	Abraham Swan, *A Collection of Designs in architecture* (2 vols., London, 1757).
British Architecture 1. –. 0	do. :	Abraham Swan, *The British Architect: or, the builder's treasury of staircases* (London, 1745).
Ware's Architecture 2. –. 0	do. :	Isaac Ware, *A Complete Body of Architecture* (2 vols., London, 1756).
Gibb's rules for drawing 1. 1. 0	do. :	James Gibbs, *Rules for drawing the several parts of architecture* (London, 1732).

Inigo Jones Architecture of : Inigo Jones, *The designs of Inigo Jones,*
Whitehall   2 designs   *consisting of plans and elevations for*
3. 0. 0   *public and private buildings. Published*
                                   by William Kent, with additional de-
                                   signs.... (2 vols., London, 1727).

Kent's design Houghton Hall : Isaac Ware, William Kent, and Thomas
1 1. 0. 0   Ripley, *The Plans...of Houghton in*
                                Norfolk,...Delineated by I. Ware and
                                W. Kent.... (London, 1735).

Swan's Carpentry 1 – 12. –   : Abraham Swan, *Designs in Carpentry*
                                   (London, 1759).

Morriss Architecture 1 – 18. – : Robert Morris, *In defence of ancient*
                                   architecture (1728).

Wm. Halfpenny's Architecture : William Halfpenny, *Practical Architec-*
1 1. 0. 0   *ture* (London, 1724); *The Art of Sound*
Half penny Architecture pam-   *Building* (London, 1725); *A New and*
phlet 0. 6. –   *Complete System of Architecture*
Half penny Architecture paste- (London, 1749); *Useful Architecture*
board – 10. –   (London, 1751); *Rural Architec-*
Half penny Architecture Quarto *ture* (London, 1752); *The Modern*
– 8. –   *Builder's Assistant* (London, 1752);
Half penny do.   *New Designs for Chinese Temples*
do. – 12. –   (London, 1750-52).
Half penny do. do. – 10. –   These appeared as pamphlets in paper
Half penny do. do. – 12. –   covers, and, like many books on car-
                                pentry, these "numbers" were later
                                bound.

Pain's Architecture & Joiner 1 : William Pain, *Builder's Companion* (Lon-
1. 0. 0   don, 1759).

Evelyn's Architecture 1 – 12.– : John Evelyn (translator), *Fréart de*
                                Chambray's Parallel of the ancient
                                architecture with the modern (London,
                                1707).

Copland's Ornaments do. 1 vol. : H. Copland, *A New Book of Ornaments*
0. 5. –   *by H. Copland* (London, 1746).

Sammon's Art of building – 12. – : William Salmon, *Palladio Londinensis, or,*
                                the London Art of Building (London,
                                1734).

Le Clerk's Architecture – 12. – : Sebastien Le Clerc, *A Treatise of Architecture* (2 vols., London, 1732).

Morris Archite. Quarto – 8. – : Robert Morris, *Select Architecture* (London, 1757).

Overt do. do. – 12. – : Thomas C. Overton, *Original designs of temples and other ornamental buildings. . . .* (London, 1766).

Art of drawing do. – 4. 6 : There were several works with this title issued in the eighteenth century.

Morris Architecture do. part : Robert Morris, *Select Architecture* (London, 1757).
– 12. –

Harmony of Building do. – 1. – : John Gwyn, *An essay upon Harmony as it relates chiefly to situation and building* (London, 1739).

Hoppus Architecture – 18. – : Edward Hoppus, *Andrea Palladio's Architecture in four books, . . . revis'd . . . by E. Hoppus* (2 vols., London, 1735, 1736).

Le Clerc Drawing – 10. – : Sebastien Le Clerc, *Les vrais principes du dessein suivis du Caractère des Passions* (Paris, 1680). Harrison's copy was an English translation that I have been unable to trace.

Inigo Jones Architecture Quarto : Isaac Ware, *Designs of Inigo Jones and others* (London, 1735).
– 15. –

An Inventory of the Estate of Peter Harrison, Esqr.
late of New Haven deceased

1 New beavor Hat		£1.10.
1 Grey buckled Wig		1.10. 0
2 Cambrick Caps	at 3/	0. 6. 0
9 Diaper Caps	at 3/	1. 7. 0
6 New Shirts	at 17/6	5. 5. 6
5 do. ruffled	at 22/	5.10. 0
6 do. half worn	at 10/	3. 0. 0
5 fine muslin Cravats	at 20/	5. 0. 0
8 old Do.	at 3/	1. 4. 0
1 Bath coating Surtout		1.10. 0
1 Plaid Gown		1. 8. 0
1 Superfine broad cloth Coat black		2. 0. 0
1 Superfine Do. Do.		3.10. 0
I Coating Coat mixt		2. 0. 0
1 Brown Sagathee Coat		0.10. 0
1 Old broad Cloth Coat		0. 6. 0
1 Old Coating Coat (mix'd)		0. 4. 6
1 White coating Coat		0.12. 0
1 Suit Green broad Cloth, Coat Vest & breeches		2. 8. 0
1 Black silk ducape Vest		2.10. 9
1 Do. Princes Stuff		2. 8. 1
1 Scarlet Whitney Vest		1.16. 0

1 Damascus Vest		£0. 8. 0
1 do. do.		10. 0
1 Do. Do. check'd		18. 0
1 black rattenet Vest		14.
1 black Sagathee do.		5.
1 do. everlasting do.		7.
2 Scarlet Vests		8.
1 pr. new Silk breeches		1.18. 0
1 pr. Do.	30/	1.10. 0
1 pr. do. princes Stuff		1. 5. 4
1 pr. Nankeen Do.		5.
1 pr. Silk Sagathee do.		5.
1 pr. new black Sattanet do.		1. 7. 3
1 pr. blk lasting do.		4.
1 pr. blk Sattanet do.		1. 5. 4
1 pr. do. Do. do.		5.
1 pr. wilton do.		9.
1 pr. Sattanet do.		5.
6 pocket handrs.	at 3/	18.
2 pr. white ribb'd worsted Hose	at 12/	1. 4. 0
2 pr. Linnen & Silk	at 8/	16.
2 pr. Cotton ribb'd do.	at 7/	0.14.
2 pr. black worsted do.	at 9/	18.
1 pr. black Silk do.		12.
1 pr. fine grey ribbs	at 10/	10.
5 pr. hemp do.	at 2/6	12. 6
3 pr. worsted ribbed & plain	at 2/6	7. 6
4 pr. Shoes	at 3/	12.
1 Cloak		5.
1 pr. half Boots		8.
1 pr. Silver Shoe buckles		
1 pr. knee do.		7.
1 pr. agate Buttons		5.
1 pr. Stone buttons		0. 7. 0
8 Mahogany Chairs	at 30/	12. 0. 0
2 Mahogany square Tables	at 72/	7. 4.
1 do. Stand		3.10.
1 ditto Tea Table		2.
2 Large looking Glasses eagld. & gilt		10.

1 compleat Sett of gilt China		£21. 0.
1 Mahogany Tea Chest		12.
1 Square Tea Board		3.
1 large round do.		9.
1 Tea Server do.		4.
1 Small ditto		2. 6
6 Gilt Pictures	at 18/	5. 8. 0
3 ditto	at 9/	1. 7. 0
1 ditto	at 12/	12. 0
1 pr. brass Andirons Tongs, Shovel & Poker		1.16. 0
1 pr. Shovel & Tongs do. brass		7.
1 pr. do. do.		6.
1 pr. do. Iron & Poker		6.
1 Hearth Brush		2. 9
1 pr. old Shovel & Tongs		2. 6
1 pr. large brass Andirons		2. 5.
1 pr. do. small		1.10.
1 pr. do high Tippd brass		12.
1 pr. Iron do. for Spit		12.
1 pr. do. small		1. 6
1 pr. Kitchen Tongs & Shovel		6.
1 pr. small do.		1. 6
2 pencild Pictures	at 45/	4.10. 0
1 large Oval Mahogany Table		2.10. 0
1 Small do. do.		1.10. 0
1 Stand do. do.		1. 5. 0
4 Bottle Stands Mahogany	at 1/6	6.
6 black walnut Chairs leather botd		3. 0. 0
8 Windsor Chairs	at 12/	4.16.
1 large long looking Glass walnut Frame gilt and shell'd		3. 0. 0
1 Large Book Case		5.10. 0
3 Check'd draw window Curtains		3.10. 0
1 hearth Brush		1.10
7 Cloak Pins	at 6d	3. 6
1 pr. brass nossle Bellows		3.
1 pr. Brass fire Tongs & Shovel Hooks		3.
6 black Chairs	at 3/	18.
4 old leather Chairs	at 4/6	10.
1 Square cherry tree Table		1. 0. 0

1 round Stand do.		£0.13.	
1 Old dressing Table		6.	
1 old walnut framd looking Glass		10.	
1 warming Pan		12.	
1 pr. neats leather bellows		4.	
10 Short Guns	at 20/	10. 0. 0	
10 Cutlasses	at 12/	6. 0. 0	
3 pr. Pistols	at 36/	5. 8.	
1 pr. pocket pistols			
1 Shagreen casd. Watch		2.10. 0	
1 Large roman Picture		1. 0	
2 Crookd. back bark bottd. Chairs	4/6	9.	
1 Large book Case		2. 0. 0	
1 pr. Bellows		2. 6	
1 Fender Iron		10.	
1 Green China Bed furniture & Bedstead		48. 0. 0	
Bed upon the same with Bolsters & Pillows		6.10.	
5 Beds ditto with Pillows &c.	at 100/	25. 0. 0	
1 Mahogany dressing Table		2.10. 0	
1 ditto Case drawers		7.10.	
6 Crook back'd green bottomd Chairs	at 16/	4.16.	
1 China Easy Chair		1. 5.	
1 Half round dressing Glass		12.	
1 Gilt shell looking Glass with Sconces		2. 5. 0	
3 pr. Green China Window Curtains	at 8/	1. 4.	
1 Hearth brush		1. 6	
6 Crook back'd Leather Chairs	at 4/6	1. 7.	
1 Broad looking Glass black walnut frame		1.15. 0	
1 Small long dressing Glass		5. 0	
1 White pine writing Desk & Chair		1.10. 0	
1 Merchants book Case		4. 0	
1 Twilight Table		1. 6	
3 Draw Tammy window Curtains Cords & Tassells	at 20/	3. 0. 0	
6 Cloak Pins	at 6d	3. 0	
2 Glass brass Pins		. 8	
1 Maple & black walnut bedstead & Sacking		12. 0	
1 Pallett bedstead		1.10. 0	
1 Cott Bedstead bottom		16. 0	

1 Hearth brush		£0. 0. 0
2 Sealskin Trunks	at 20/	2. 0. 0
2 blk. leather do.	at 12/	1. 4.
1 Turkey leather do.	9/	9.
1 do. do. Small	5/	5.
1 small black do.	10/	10.
2 large black do.	at 12/	1. 4.
1 Pipe & Tabor		1.10. 0
1 bedstead & Sacking		1. 0. 0
2 old Chests		4. 0
1 pr. Bellows neats leather		5. 0
2 Checkd window Curtains	at 10/	1. 0. 0
3 pr. brass hinges		4. 6
2 pr. small do.		2. 4
1 Iron Fender		6.
1 black Tin Ink Stand		2.
5 Shoe brushes		2.
5 Chest Locks		10.
6 Window Curtain Hooks	at 6d	3.
9 Brass weights		16.
Negro Man Apollo & bed		30. 0. 0
Negro Woman Lucy & beding		40. 0. 0
1 Pillion		10.
1 Horse Collar		4.
1 Great Wheel		5.
1 Reel clock work		5.
1 large Iron fender		15.
2 Garden Rakes		1. 2
2 Dung forks	at 2/6	5.
1 black Arm Chair		3.
2 Boxes for making Candles		8.
1 Saddle hog skin seat, & bridle		2.14.
1 Do. quilted Seat & bridle		5. 8.
2 Clothes Baskets	at 1/3	3.
1 Coverd. Do.		2.
2 Wicker Do.	at 1/6	3.
1 Hair cloth Line		6.
1 Large wicker basket		6.
1 Small square do.		4.

1 round basket		£0. 2. 6
6 Do. with handle	at 1/6	9. 0
1 Chintz Gown 10 yd.	at 5/	2.10. 0
1 Curricle & Harness compleat		48. 0. 0
1 Chaise & Harness		14. 0. 0
1 Wheel barrow		15. 0
1 large bay horse sold		24. 0. 0
1 Ditto		24. 0. 0
1 Cow		4.10. 0
20 doz. black qt. bottles	at 3/9	3.15. 0
3 doz. 2 qt. do.		1. 2. 6
2 5 Gallon Do.	at 10/	1.
1 Handsaw		10.
1 Scale Beam		6.
5 Augers	at 10d	4. 2
8 Gimlets		1. 6
1 Tap bore		4
4 Chisels & 1 Gouge		3. 4
2 draw Shaves		3.
1 Coopers Adds		1. 6
Staples Nails and old Iron		1. 6
Plains and Irons		2. 0
2 Hammers & hatchets		1. 6
6 Twine	at 9d	4. 6
12 old Pictures		5.
2 Glass lignum vita Ink Stands	at 1/	2. 0
60 ½ Pewter	at 1/3	3.15.7½
2 Brass Kettles wt. 35	at 1/8	2.18. 4
1 Large brass Skillet & frame & Cover		17.
1 do. smaller		12. 0
1 do. do.		3. 6
1 Iron Skillet		1. 4
1 Broad copper sauce pan		1. 0. 0
1 Tea Kettle		18. 0
1 High copper stew Pan		16. 0
1 Copper Coffee Pot		9. 0
1 ditto old		4.
1 Copper chocolate Pot		16.
1 Large baking copper Pan		6.

1 Smaller	do.		£0. 4. 6
1 Copper butter Pan			2. 6
1 2 qt. copper Pot			5. 0
1 pint	do.		3. 0
1 Copper fish Kettle			2.14. 0
1 Plated iron sauce Pan			2. 6
1 Copper baking Pan			1.16. 0
2 Brass chafing dishes		at 5/	10. 0
1 Bell metal mortar sold			3. 2. 6
1 Brass flower Box			2. 6
1 Pepper	do.		1. 6
1 Brass Scimmer			2. 6
1 do. Ladle			2.
1 Flesh Fork			3.
1 pr. Brass Scales			3.
2 pr. Brass Candelsticks		at 8/	16.
1 do. single			3.
1 Pr. flat bottomd. Candlesticks brass		12/	0.12. 0
1 pr. Smaller	do.	5/	5. 0
1 do. single			1. 6
1 Brass Snuffer Stand			1. 6
4 Iron Candlesticks		at 6d	2. 0
1 Cheese Toaster			1. 6
1 Large Tin Funnel			1. 8
1 Small tin do.			9
1 Large Tin Cover			2. 0
2 Smaller do.		at 8d.	1. 4
1 Tin Oven			8. 0
1 do. Candle Box			3. 0
1 Apple Toaster			2. 6
6 Candle Molds			3. 6
2 Graters			6
2 Tin Custard Pans		at 1/6	3. 0
3 Small do		at 10d	2. 6
1 Cheese Toaster			1. 0
12 Round dish Patty Pans			2. 0
12 Smaller	do.		1. 6
6 small scollopd.	Do.		1. 0
16 do.	do.		1. 4

1 Doz. pewter Candle molds fluted		£0.18. 0
2 Large Spits		6. 0
1 Small Do.		1. 6
1 Small Churn		2. 0
Wooden Bowls		0. 7
1 Bread Tray		2. 6
1 Knife Box		1. 6
10 Stone Pickle Pots	at 1/6	15. 0
2 Butter Tubs	at 3/	6. 0
1 Hair Sieve		1. 0
1 Piggen		1. 0
1 Lignum V. Mortar		4. 0
1 Warming Pan		9.
2 Tin Water Pots	at 3/	6.
1 Wood Saw		4.
2 Falling Axes	at 5/	10.
1 pr. Bellows in Kitchen	at 1/8	1. 8
1 Large gridiron		8. 0
1 Smaller do.		2. 0
7 Scewers & hanger		1. 8
5 Sad Irons		9. 2
1 Large Box Iron		3. 0
1 Small do.		3. 0
1 Pr. Steel yards		10. 0
1 Tin Chane		2. 0
1 Tin Lanthorn		3. 0
1 Glass Do.		8.
1 Iron Pan fender		2.
1 Iron harts		1.
1 Saw Trammel		6.
1 do. common		6.
1 Iron Tea Kettle		6.
1 Spider		4.
1 Iron bake Pan		5.
1 Large Iron Pot bail & Cover	55	8.
1 Smaller do.	21	3.
1 Smaller do. & hooks		3.
1 do. do. & hooks		3.
1 do. Dish Kettle		4.

1 Small Spider		£0. 1.
1 Pudding Kettle		0. 2. 0
1 Small disk Kettle		1. 8
1 frying Pan		5. 0
1 Iron Bason		1. 9
1 Spade		5. 9
1 Ditching Spade		1. 6
1 Half Bushel		2. 0
2 Oak washing Tubs	at 3/4	6. 8
3 Water Pails	at 1/	3. 0
7 White Kitchen Chairs	at 1/8	11. 8
2 White Kitchen Tables	at 2/6	5. 0
1 Ditto framed		5.
2 Benches		2.
1 Bread Board		1. 7
6 Cyder Barrells	at 2/	12. 0
4 Meat Tierces	at 6/	1. 4. 0
1 pr. neat Spring Snuffers polished		8.
1 pr. ditto springd		2.
1 Carving knife & fork		6.
12 large Ivory knives & forks do.		2. 8.
10 ditto smaller knives & forks		10.
1 doz. china		18.
1 Doz. buck horn do.		8.
1 Stone soap dish		2.
8 do. Plates	at 6d	4.
2 ditto	at 6d	1.
14 Common ditto	at 5d	5.10
5 Butter plates	at 4d	1. 8
1 Large stone platter		4.
1 do. 3/6 do. 3/ do 2.6 do 2/		11.
2 ditto	at 1/6	3.
1 Large oval Platter		0. 4. 0
1 Do. smaller		3. 0
11 Stone baking Pans	at 8d	7. 4
1 Large delph Bowl		3. 6
2 Large stone Pitchers		3. 0
1 Smaller do.		5
1 Stone Coffee Pot		1. 0

1 do. Tea Pot		£0.10
1 Delph Platter		1. 6
6 Plates do.		6. 0
12 Common stone Plates		4. 6
1 Large stone Pitcher		1. 6
1 Smaller do.		9
1 large Stone Pot		1. 6
2 Do. Quart		1. 4
2 do. cream cold. Pots	1/	2. 0
1 pint do. do.		8
3 Potting Pins	at 6d	1. 6
8 Cream cold. Bowls	at 6d	4.
2 Butter Boats	at 8d	1. 4
2 butter Boats larger	8/	2. 0
1 Mustard Pot	6d	6
1 Milk Pot	6	6
2 small Pitchers	8d	1. 4
2 Cream cold. Tea Pots	at 1/4	2. 8
1 Painted do.		
1 Pencil painted Tea Pot	2/	2.
1 Set cream cold. Tea Cups & Saucers	1/2	1. 2
3 Cake Pans	6d	0. 6
1 Stone strainer	1/	1. 0
1 Cream cold. Sugar Dish	1/	1. 0
1 Cream Pot	6d	6
1 Delph Plate	10d	10
2 Stone Sauce Pans	at 8	1. 4
2 Delph Butter Boats	at 1/4	2. 8
1 Cream Pail		3
1 Small Porringer and Bowl		5
2 red China Tea Pots	at 2/	4. 0
1 Large milk pot do.		1. 0
2 Sugar Dishes do.	at 8d	1. 4
1 Bowl do.	1/	1. 0
1 Milk Pot do.		10
1 Small White Stone Tea Pot	7d	7
1 Agate Sugar dish	10d	10
1 Cream cold. do.	6d	6
1 do. milk Pot	4d	4
1 do. Bowl	3d	3

1 ½ doz. wine glasses	at 16/	£1. 4. 0
1 Cut Decanter	5/	5. 0
2 Do. common	3/	6. 0
3 Wine & Water Glasses		6. 0
2 Tall Beer Glasses		5. 0
2 do. do.	at 1/3	2. 6
2 Glass Casters	at 3/	6. 0
7 Wormed Wine glasses	at 1/4	9. 4
1 Japann'd board		5. 0
4 doz. Jelly Glasses	at 4/	16. 0
1 Compleat Set black Ware	18/	18. 0
54 ½ doz. Penknives	at 3/9	10. 5.10
1 Silver Coffee Pot 30 oz.		13. 0. 0
1 Do. Tea Pot 17 oz. pt.		7. 0. 0
9 do. Table Spoons 15.5		6. 4. 2
15 do. Tea Spoons & Tea Tongs 5.15		2.17.10
1 pr. Silver Candlesticks		6. 0. 0
3 China Dishes	at 12/	1.16. 0
2 Oval Soup do.	at 12/	1. 4. 0
2 flat small do.	at 6/	12. 0
9 baking Dishes do.	at 6/	2.14. 0
2 Punch Bowls do.	at 12/	1. 4. 0
2 doz. China Plates	at 36/	3.12. 0
10 China Butter Plates	at 1/6	15. 0
1 doz. China Patty Pans	at 24/	1. 4. 0
2 China butter Boats	at 4/	8. 0
6 Custard Cups	at 1/	6. 0
6 Square patty pans	at 1/6	9.
6 China blue & white Cups & Saucers	7/	7.
1 Sett burnt China gilt Cups & Saucers		10.
2 Sets blue & white do.		12.
1 Set Coffee Cups & Saucers		10.
1 burnt China Punch bowl	at 18/	18.
1 do. mended		12.
7 Brown China Custard Cups	at 1/6	10. 6
7 Pint China Gilt Bowls	at 3/	1. 1. 0
2 do. Smaller	at 1/6	3.
1 Small Tea Pot do.	2/	2.
1 Small Canister do.	2/	2.
1 old flint frame Caster	40/	2. 0. 0

1 Toasting fork	2/	£0. 2.	
6 larding Pins	at 1/	6.	
13 Pr. Sheets	at 20/	13. 0. 0	
3 Damask Table Cloths	at 40/	6. 0. 0	
1 Doz. Napkins do.	50/	2.10. 0	
1 Diaper Table Cloth	at 16/	16. 0	
4 do. do.	at 12/	2. 8. 0	
4 small do.	at 4/	16. 0	
13 Diaper Towels	at 1/	13. 0	
6 pr. fine holland pillow Coats	at 8/	2. 8. 0	
4 pr. do.	at 6/	1. 4. 0	
1 pr. fine do.	7/	7. 0	
6 pr. do.	at 4/	1. 4. 0	
12 Tow Towels	at 9d	9.	
1 Cotton Counterpin	160/	8. 0. 0	
1 Counterpin		1.10. 0	
1 Chintz Counterpin		9.	
9 yds. furniture Check Counterpin		1. 7. 0	
1 Green Rugg	30/	1.10. 0	
1 Small do.	15/	15.	
1 pr. Rose blankets	36/	1.16. 0	
1 pr. Do.	24/	1. 4. 0	
1 pr. do.	20/	1. 0. 0	
4 pr. do. old	at 16/	3. 4. 0	
1 pr. old do.	10/	10.	
1 Pocket Lanthorn		12.	
2 Leathern Buckets and bags	at 7/	14.	
1 Tin Stove		3.	
1 Safe		8.	
1 56 Iron weight		6.	
2 28 do.		6.	
2 14 do.		3.	
1 Short spy Glass brass case		3. 0. 0	
1 long cane Do.		0.10. 0	
1 Italian painted Crucifix		20. 0. 0	
1 do. St. Francis		13. 0. 0	
2 Cast steel rasors Strops & hone		17. 0	
1 Set Shoe & knee pinchbeck buckles		1. 4. 0	
1 Silver stock buckle		3. 0	

FIGURES 15-16. Introduction of the Palladian style to America, 1749. (*Above*) The façade, or west end, of the Redwood Library at Newport, designed by Peter Harrison after popular English models that derived their inspiration from Palladio. Harrison was one of the first American designers to produce a resemblance to rusticated stonework in wood, and his success in working out a whole system of rustic work is clearly shown in this structure. (*Below*) One of the designs then in vogue in England, from the Fourth Book of *Andrea Palladio's Architecture* (1736), by Edward Hoppus, a copy of which was in Peter Harrison's library. See Appendix C.

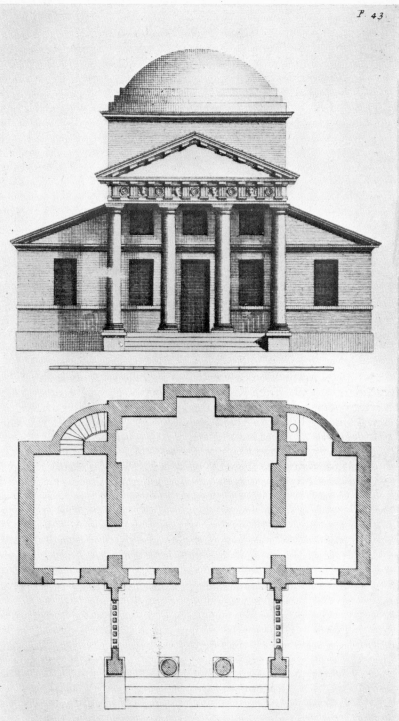

W. Kent inv.   I. Ware Delin.   P. Fourdrinier Sculp.

Extends 115 feet

FIGURE 17. (*On facing page*) This garden pavilion, designed by William Kent for Sir Charles Hotham and published by Isaac Ware in *Designs of Inigo Jones and others* (1735), Plate 43, not only supplied Harrison with an elevation but furnished a plan which he followed rather literally in the Redwood Library. This source was published a year earlier than the one in Figure 16, and Harrison owned them both. See Appendix C.

FIGURE 18. (*Above*) The west front of the Church of Santo Giorgio at Venice, by Palladio, was the ultimate source of Peter Harrison's façade for the Redwood Library. It was published by William Kent as Plate 59 of the first volume of his *Designs of Inigo Jones* (1727, reprinted 1833). Harrison owned this volume. See Appendix C.

FIGURES 19-20. Among the sources for Harrison's treatment of the rear façade (now on the side) of the Redwood Library, shown at left, were: (1) a building of the Earl of Burlington at Chiswick in William Kent's *Designs of Inigo Jones* (1727, reprinted 1833), Volume I, Plate 73, shown below, and (2) the Headpiece to the Fourth Book of Edward Hoppus, *Andrea Palladio's Architecture* (1736.) Both of these are listed in Harrison's inventory. See Appendix C.

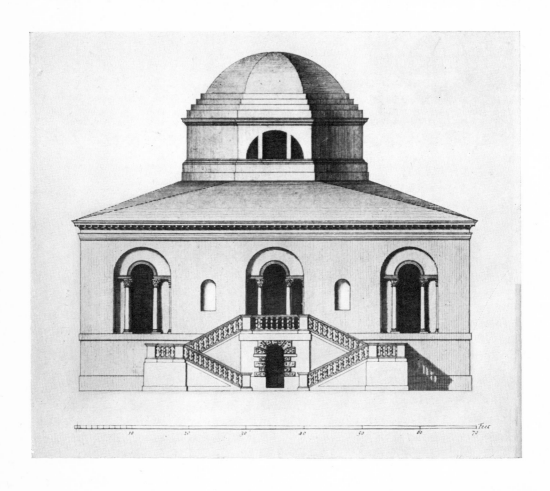

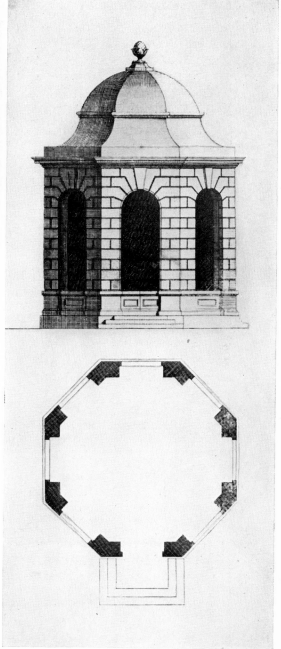

FIGURES 21-22. (*Above*) Summer House for Abraham Redwood's estate, but since moved to the Redwood Library grounds, which Peter Harrison took directly from a plate (*right*) in his copy of James Gibbs, *A Book of Architecture* (1728), Plate 80. See Appendix C.

FIGURES 23-24. King's Chapel, designed in 1749 and under construction from 1750 to 1758, was Peter Harrison's masterpiece even though it was never completed according to his drawings. He skillfully employed a design for the exterior and planned a tower more elaborate than any in London—the whole constituting a notable advance in American church architecture. For the plan, as well as the body of the edifice, he leaned heavily upon the designs (*below*) for Marylebone Church in his copy of James Gibbs, *A Book of Architecture* (1728), Plate 24. See Appendix C.

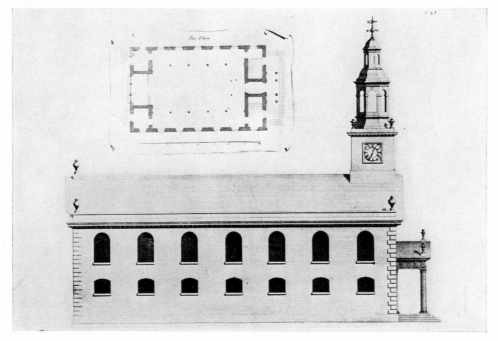

FIGURE 25. Interior of King's Chapel, showing Peter Harrison's employment of double Corinthian columns to support a vaulted ceiling over the aisles, and a nicely designed altarpiece surmounted by a Palladian window in the curved apse. The Venetian window is in the manner of James Gibbs and could have been suggested to Harrison by Plates 4 and 27 of the copy of *A Book of Architecture* (1728) in his collection. See Appendix C.

FIGURE 26. St. Michael's in Charles Town, South Carolina, 1751-1761, was probably designed by Peter Harrison, although changes were made in the portico before construction began. The plan was said to have been taken from Gibbs, but does not conform at all closely to any one of his churches. The rustication around the base of the tower, the windows, and the doors was a feature of several of Harrison's buildings. St. Michael's and King's Chapel were the only churches designed in the colonies that had a porch the full height of the building.

FIGURE 27. West front of the Jewish Synagogue at Newport, erected 1759-1763, showing at the left the school house that Harrison was forced to attach on the north side. Because the temple had to be placed at an angle on the lot so that the Ark might face due east, the school is fortunately not visible from the street. The edifice lacks a beautiful cornice that was removed in the nineteenth century.

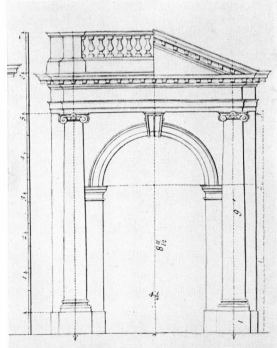

FIGURE 28. The porch of Peter Harrison's Synagogue at Newport.

FIGURE 29. A possible inspiration for the Synagogue porch from one of Harrison's books: James Gibbs, *Rules for Drawing* (1738), Plate 39, Figure 3. See Appendix C.

FIGURE 30. The exquisite interior of Peter Harrison's Synagogue closely resembles the
Sephardic Synagogue at Amsterdam, Holland, in plan. (See Figure 31) Its most arresting feature is the Anglican architect's excellent solution for the Ark at the east end, which he arrived
at by combining two designs by Kent and one by Batty Langley. (See Figures 33-35)

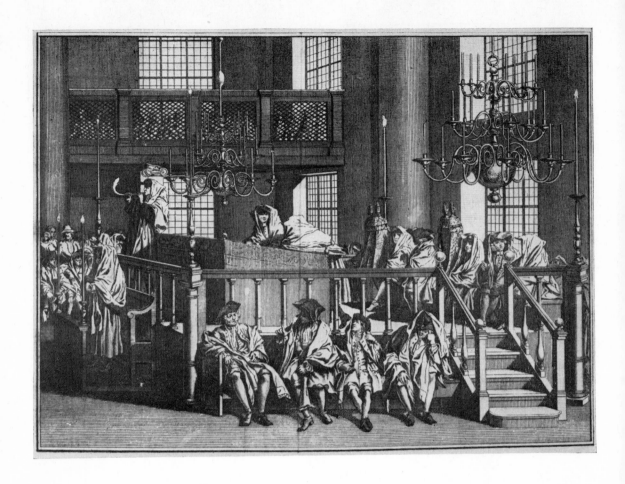

FIGURES 31-32. Sources for the plan of the Newport Synagogue. (*Above*) the interior of the Synagogue at Amsterdam, showing the traditional arrangement for worship according to the Sephardic ritual, with a gallery for the women, from the *Gentleman's Magazine* (1788), p. 200. (*Right*) John Webb's design for a chapel at Whitehall that Harrison found in his edition of William Kent's *Designs of Inigo Jones* (1727, reprinted 1833), Volume I, Plate 50. See Appendix C.

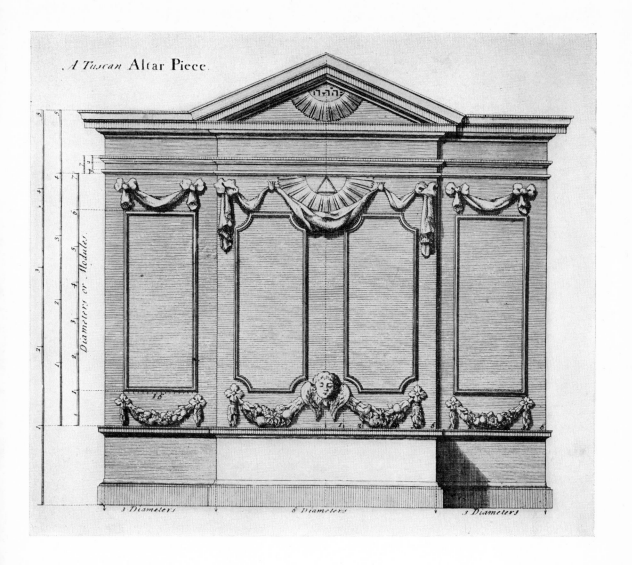

A Tuscan Altar Piece.

FIGURES 33-35. The solution Peter Harrison created for the Ark of the Newport Synagogue (see Figure 30). (*On facing page*) Two chimney pieces by William Kent which Harrison combined for the upper part of the Ark. They are to be found in his copies of Isaac Ware, *Designs of Inigo Jones and others* (1735), Plate 48, and William Kent, *Designs of Inigo Jones* (1727, reprinted 1833), Volume I, Plate 63. (*Above*) A Tuscan altarpiece from Batty Langley, *A Treasury of Designs* (1740), Plate 108, was the basis for his treatment of the lower part of the Ark. See Appendix C.

FIGURES 36-37. (*On facing page*) The Brick Market at Newport, 1761-1772, Peter Harrison's last and most academic building. Knowing that his fellow-townsmen expected a structure resting on arches like any English market house, he turned to his *Vitruvius Britannicus* (1715-1725) and found a suitable design on Plate 16 of Volume I, the great gallery at Somerset House (*above*). See Appendix C.

FIGURE 38. Christ Church at Cambridge, Massachusetts, 1760-1761, the most personal of Peter Harrison's designs. The specifications called for the "Building to be of wood, and covered on the outside with Rough-cast;" but no plaster was ever applied because of the expense. Although the Vestry did not want a spire, there is some evidence that the architect planned one that was never erected.

FIGURE 39. The north side of Christ Church, showing the heavy, fully-membered, Doric cornice and the pleasant-appearing window arches with imposts and archivolts. Had the rough-cast finish been applied to the wood facing, as planned, a definite impression of a stone structure would have been created.

FIGURES 40-41. The interior of Christ Church, looking toward the west end. The beautifully proportioned balcony over the entrance, which is reminiscent of a triumphal arch, seems to come from a design Harrison found in his oft-consulted *Rules for Drawing* (1738), Plate 36, just as Plate 2 of Gibbs could have supplied the model for the large Ionic columns. See Appendix C.

CONTRACT [1]

I. Erection of Library Building

Articles of Agreement Indented made and concluded upon the ninth Day of August in the twenty-second year of his Majesty's Reign. George the second, King of Great Britain &c. Anno Dominie One Thousand seven Hundred and forty-eight, Between Wing Spooner, Samuel Green, Thomas Melvil and Israel Chapman, all of Newport, in the County of Newport and Colony of Rhode Island, House Carpenters, of the One Part, And Samuel Wickham, Esq., Henry Collins and John Tillinghast, Merchants, all of Newport aforesaid, Three of the Directors of the Redwood Library in Newport, aforesaid, of the other part: Witness, That the said Wing Spooner, Samuel Green, Thomas Melvil and Israel Chapman, Do hereby Covenant, Promise and Engage to Erect and build in Newport aforesaid, on the Lott of Land given by said Henry Collins of that purpose a House or Building to be called the Redwood Library, suitable and convenient for depositing therein a large number of books given by Abraham Redwood, Esq., for Public use: That is to say, to do and perform all the Carpenters and House joyners Work in and about said House of the following Dimensions and in the manner hereinafter express'd, Viz: The large Room to be thirty-seven foot long, and twenty-six foot broad in the inside, and nineteen foot high. At the west End (which is the Principal Front) is to be a Portico of four Columns accord-

[1] George C. Mason, *Annals of the Redwood Library*, 488-91.

ing to the Dorick Order, with a Pediment over it, with Pilasters to suit the Columns. The Projection of the Portico from the Outside of the Building to be about nine foot, and the Roof to be continued out so much as to form the Pediment: The length of the Columns to be about seventeen foot including Base and Capital, and the thickness of twenty-six inches just above the Base: The Building to be fram'd Brac'd and Studded the outside and Roof to be boarded with Feather edg'd Boards, the Shingles to be shav'd and joynted and to be laid: The outside to be covered with Pine Plank worked in Imitation of Rustick, and to have a Dorick Entablature with Triglipphs &c. continued from the Portico quite Round the Building and to have a Plain Pediment at the East End. At the West End next the Portico, to be two small Wings or Outshots for two Little Rooms or offices, one on each side and both alike in form and Bigness, each to be about twelve foot square and (with a small Break or Recess) to Range in a line Parallel to the West End of the Building or inner part of the Portico. The Roofs of these Outshots to be Slooping from the lower part of the Entablature so as to form a Kind of half Pediment on each Side of the Portico, with a Cornice only to be work'd round instead of the whole Entablature, the height of them to be about eleven foot at the outer-most Side and seventeen foot at the Inner side or where they joyn the Body of the Building, and to be plank'd as the other in Imitation of the Rustick: in the Front of said Building to be four whole windows and two Attic windows, on each side four whole windows and three attic windows: In all Twelve whole Windows and nine Attick Windows: The whole Windows to be six foot high and three foot wide, and the Attick Windows to be three foot square within the Frames, of which are to be red cedar and quite plain without any Architrave on the Outside. At the East end to have a Venetian Window only: To Have three outside doors, Viz., One large One in the middle of the Portico, eight foot six Inches high and three foot nine inches wide, and two Small ones in the back part of the two Outshots, and to have four Inside Doors, to consist of eight Pannels each and cas'd with Double Architrave. The Sides and Ends of the Great Room within to be furr'd out even with the Posts, and the ceiling to be furr'd out with a small Cove next the Walls about two foot Downwards at the Bottom of which over the Attick Windows and Ionick Cornice to run quite round: To be wainscotted about five foot high from the floor quite round the great Room: The Jambs of the Windows to be wainscotted With Architraves round and Seats in the lower Windows: within Great Door which is

the entrance from the Portico a small [obliterated] is to be partitioned
off for a Porch with a door on the inside and therein to erect a small
Plain Stair Case, to go up to the Roof of the Building. The Floors to be
laid with Plank Rabbitted or with Double Boards. About four foot from
the Walls or Sides of the Great Room must be a sort of Partition erected
about ten feet high, with openings over against each window, on both
Sides of which must be placed Shelves for the Books; there must also
be five or six Desks for laying the Books on in convenient Places, and
the whole to be finished and compleated well and workmanlike according to a Plan or Draught drawn by Mr. Joseph Harrison, and agreed
on for that Purpose, On or before the last Day of October, which will
be in the year of our Lord One Thousand Seven Hundred and forty-
nine. For and in Consideration whereof the said Samuel Wickham, Henry
Collins and John Tillinghast Do hereby Covenant, Promist and Engage
to pay or cause to be paid to the sd Wing Spooner, Samuel Green,
Thomas Melvil and Israel Chapman for sd Work the Sum of two Thousand and two Hundred pounds in good and passable Bills of Publick
Credit of sd Colony, old Tenor; Six Hundred pounds thereof when the
Roof is shingled, and the Remainder when the Building is finished; and
to find and provide for the carrying on and finishing said Building all
the Stuff and materials needful and necessary as the same shall be wanted.
And for the true performance of these Articles and every clause thereof,
the said Parties Bind themselves each to the other joyntly and severally
firmly by these presents in the penal sum of Four Thousand Pounds,
Current passable Bills of Public Credit of said Colony, Old Tenor, to
be forfeited and paid by the Party failing to the other Party.

In Witness whereof, the Parties to these presents have hereunto interchangeably Set their hands and Seals the Day and year first above
written.

ARTICLES

II. For Building the Library

Memorandum: That the Parties to the within written Articles of
Agreement, notwithstanding what is therein written, Do hereby agree
to the following alterations in that building therein mentioned upon the
same penalty as within, viz., that the four Pilasters in the front of the

House, all the windows in the north and South West of said House: the stair case and Partitions within side, the Venitian Window in the East End, and the wainscott on the north and south Side within the House, as far as the Shelves extend, be all omitted, and that instead of the Venitian Window in the East end, there be three small Windows, that the Shelves for the Books be placed against the Walls of the Building, that there be a stair case at the west end of sd House, the Ceiling of the Portico to have a cornice and that the Planshear and Entablature and all other Parts of said Building be finished and compleated well and workmanlike agreeable to a plan or Draught drawn by Mr. Peter Harrison, and all Parts of the within mentioned Articles of agreement to stand good excepting such alterations as are made by this Additional agreement, And in Consideration of the Builders Conforming to ye sd Draught drawn by Mr. Peter Harrison, and following his directions as to all the Alterations herein mentioned and all other parts of said Building according to the true Intent and meaning of said Articles, The within named Saml Wickham, Henry Collins and John Tillinghast Do hereby Oblige themselves to pay to the within-named Wing Spooner, Samuel Green, Thomas Melvil and Israel Chapman, the Sum of One Hundred pounds, old Tenor, over and above the two Thousand two hundred pounds within mentioned.

In Witness whereof the Parties to these Presents have interchangeably set their hands and seals the Sixth Day of February in the twenty second year of his Majty's Reign Anno Dominie 1748.

SAMUEL WICKHAM,
HENRY COLLINS,
JOHN TILLINGHAST.

Sign'd Seal'd and Deliver'd
  in the presence of
    SAMUEL ENGS,
    GIDEON SISSON

INDEX

Index

Acklam, Isabelle, wife of Peter Acklam, 4

Acklam, Jonathan, of Wyeston, Bawtry, England, 4-5, 7, 27, 121

Acklam, Peter, 4, 7

Adams, Samuel, 135

Agricultural interests of PH, 69

Allen, Ralph, of Bath, England, 59n., 62

Alling, Enos, 138, 139

American Philosophical Society, 140

American Society, held at Philadelphia, for Promoting Useful Knowledge, 140

Anglican church
  in New Hampshire, 142-43, 153
  in New Haven, 136-38

Apprentices, 82

Apthorp, Charles, 55

Apthorp, Rev. East, 112, 113, 115, 116

Architectural books, 39, 40, 118
  see also Library of PH—architectural books

Architectural sources of designs of PH
  see names of buildings, e.g. Redwood Library

Architectural training of PH, 2n., 38, 41, 44-45, 51n., 117-18

Architecture
  as a gentle accomplishment, 2, 37, 39, 53, 119-20
  as a profession, 2, 3, 39
  colonial, 47-48
  English, 38-39

Aristocratic ideas of PH, 5, 33, 43, 68, 74

Arnold, Benedict, 128, 146, 155

Arnold, Jonathan, 137

Arnold, Joseph, 89

Arts in America, xi

Arundel, Earl of, 37

Bagnall, Benjamin, Jr., 87

Banister, Hermione Pelham, 7, 16, 23n., 123n.

Banister, John
  acquaintance with Acklams, 7
  business with Joseph Harrison, 8-10, 13-14
  business with PH, 11-12, 15-16, 86
  comments on Harrison brothers, 8, 26,-28
  competition with House of Harrison, 30, 35
  death, 123n.
  executor of Pelham estate, 16, 27
  social status, 7n.
  trading activities, 7, 13, 36, 123n.

Banister, Thomas, father of John B., 7n.

Barney, Jacob, 139

Barzil, Philip, 148

Bawtry, England, 5

Beavertail Light, 59, 88-90
  plans by PH, 89

Bennett, John, 16

Bergen-op-Zoom, 34

Birket, James
  comments on Redwood Library, 51